ENGLAND'S UNDISCOVERED HERITAGE

ENGLAND'S UNDISCOVERED HERITAGE

A Guide to 100 Unusual Sites and Monuments

DEBRA SHIPLEY & MARY PEPLOW

An Owl Book

HENRY HOLT AND COMPANY
NEW YORK

Text copyright © 1988 by Debra Shipley and Mary Peplow
Photographs copyright © English Heritage
Design copyright © 1988 by Breslich & Foss
Published in the United States by
Henry Holt and Company, Inc., 115 West 18th Street,
New York, New York 10011.
Published in Canada by Fitzhenry & Whiteside Limited,
195 Allstate Parkway, Markham, Ontario L3R 4T8.

Library of Congress Catalog Card Number: 87-45992

ISBN 0-8050-0716-4

First American Edition

Designed and produced by
Breslich & Foss
Golden House
28-31 Great Pulteney Street
London W1R 3DD

Editor: Judy Martin
Editorial: Robert Stewart, Jim Abram, Marg Stimson
Designer: Roger Daniels
Map illustrations: Ewing Paddock Associates

Printed in Hong Kong

1   3   5   7   9   10   8   6   4   2

ISBN 0-8050-0716-4

CONTENTS

ENGLISH HERITAGE

English Heritage is the main national body responsible for the conservation of the architectural and archaeological heritage of England. It cares for nearly 400 historic properties and sites as well as advising the Government on conservation legislation and giving grants to other bodies for the care of historic buildings, historic towns, ancient monuments and rescue archaeology.

PUBLISHER'S NOTE

English Heritage has direct responsibility for over 350 sites of which 100 have been selected for this book. From time to time, it is necessary to close sites for conservation work or change opening hours for administrative reasons. A telephone contact number is provided with each entry and it is advisable to check details of opening hours, admission fees and wheelchair access before your visit.

The information panels may include details of museums with exhibits relating to certain sites. An asterisk denotes that these are not under the administration of English Heritage.

English Heritage
Fortress House
23 Savile Row
London W1X 2HE
Telephone: 01 734 6010

Author's Acknowledgements

Special thanks are due to the custodians of the many sites we visited who were enthusiastic and friendly in showing us the more unusual features and points of particular interest. We would also like to say a big thank-you to all the people who have helped with our research especially: Paul Anderson, Ilone Antoniŭs, Mike, Margaret and Richard Atkinson, Katy Carter, Cath Gould, Hotel Nelson (Norwich), Simon Molesworth, Sarah Priday.

Breslich & Foss would like particularly to thank Katy Carter, Selina Fellows, Paul Highnam, Pat Langer and Maureen Williams of English Heritage for their assistance and cooperation in preparation of this book.

INTRODUCTION

From historic houses to fantastic follies, glorious gardens to Roman remains, we were amazed at the wealth of England's heritage to be discovered everywhere from out of the way places to major town centres. We've visited all the sites in the book: some, such as Belsay Hall, Castle and Gardens, make a perfect day out for all the family; others have a particularly interesting feature, such as the wall paintings at Longthorpe Tower; all have something unusual to offer visitors.

The sites are arranged in alphabetical order for easy reference; each entry includes a description of the property, highlighting some of the more important and interesting points, and provides the exact location and directions for getting there. We have indicated the opening times, fees and wheelchair access in general terms to allow for possible administrative changes – to avoid disappointment, especially if you're travelling any distance, telephone in advance for the details you need. To help you plan your visits the back of the book contains a section recommending sites where you can picnic, or which offer entertainments and special events, and county maps showing the sites in the area.

We hope you will enjoy, as much as we have, discovering a little more of England's fascinating heritage.

Debra Shipley and Mary Peplow
September 1987

ACTON BURNELL CASTLE

Despite its name, Acton Burnell is not a castle, but a fortified manor house. There was a manor on this site grand enough to have entertained the king and parliament in 1283, and shortly afterwards it was fortified by royal licence. At this time it was the property of Robert Burnell, Chancellor of England in the reign of Edward I and also Bishop of Bath and Wells. What remains today of his castle is the shell of the central block, which contained Burnell's private lodgings, and its four rectangular towers. The great hall and chambers were on the upper floors, with servants' accommodation and storage space below. It is likely that there were many more buildings, and that the castle was protected by an outer wall and moat.

A striking view of the manor's red sandstone facade and flanking towers can be gained from the graveyard of the adjacent village church. To reach the ruins from here, you must pass through a tunnel of yews and rhododendrons, which opens out onto a cleanly shaved lawn.

A visit to Acton Burnell can be combined with one to Langley Chapel, a tiny medieval chapel which was restored in 1601 and retains wooden fittings which provide an excellent example of the layout of a seventeenth-century Puritan church. This is reached by a pleasant 1½ mile (2.4km) walk through country lanes.

SHROPSHIRE

In Acton Burnell, on unclassified road 8 miles (12.8km) south of Shrewsbury
OS map 126: ref SJ 534019
Open year round; entrance free
Wheelchair access
Tel: Area office (0902) 765105

Langley Chapel
1½ miles (2.4km) south of Acton Burnell on unclassified road off A49 9½ miles (15.2km) south of Shrewsbury
OS map: 126: ref SJ 538001
Admission by prior arrangement; entrance free
Wheelchair access
Tel: Area office (0902) 765105)

ALDBOROUGH ROMAN TOWN

The small, pretty village of Aldborough, with its traditional maypole and stocks, is built on the site of the once-prosperous Roman city of Isurium Brigantum. Its Roman origins are well concealed, though some interesting evidence of Roman occupation remains. The modern road into the village follows the Roman street plan (the west gate is thought to be underneath it) and the Roman forum, or central open space, still exists. You can also see remnants of the town wall – 8ft 6in (2.6m) wide and built of local red sandstone on a foundation of clay and cobble.

The most spectacular remains are two mosaic pavements, which are still in the original positions. The first, which shows an animal (possibly a lion or panther) under a stylized tree, bordered by a series of patterns, was found in 1832 and is slightly damaged. The second, found in 1848, is in perfect condition. This 12ft (3.6m) wide pavement is decorated with a number of alternating borders in black and white and in yellow, black and white. At its centre is an eight-pointed star. Excavations in the village have uncovered other interesting finds, some of which are on show in the small local museum. The museum houses a selection of bronze objects which show Celtic influence in their shape and design, and examples of pottery made both in Britain and abroad. There are also tiles (which were used for roofs, floors and the flues of central heating systems), glass (including a small flask with a snake-thread decoration) and a number of pins, needles and spoons made from bone.

NORTH YORKSHIRE

6 miles (9.6km) southeast of Ripon, on minor road off B6265
OS map 99: ref SE 405667
Open year round; entrance fee payable during summer
  months
Tel: Site office (09012) 2768

APPULDURCOMBE HOUSE

Appuldurcombe House, of which only the shell now stands, dates from 1701. It was built by local masons, using local stone, as a country house for Sir Robert Worsley, the fourth baronet, who inherited the family estate of Appuldurcombe. When he died in 1713, the house was still unfinished, though the east front, a fine example of English Baroque architecture was already completed.

No further work was done until 1772, when Sir Richard Worsley began to enlarge and remodel the house both inside and out. He employed the finest craftsmen, including the furniture designer, Thomas Chippendale. Sir Richard built the northwest pavilion and several other rooms, and redesigned the hall. He also had the grounds landscaped by 'Capability' Brown, whose informal design has been partially restored by a recent programme of replanting. The fountain at the entrance and the Freemantle Gate, an Ionic triumphal arch with wrought-iron gates, are believed to be the work of the eminent eighteenth-century architect, James Wyatt.

By the Porte Cochère at the rear of the building, many visitors claim to have witnessed the ghost of one of Sir Richard's lovers, whom he beat to death on discovering that she was bearing his child. Sir Richard seems to have lead a rather ill-fated life romantically. He married the beautiful Seymour Dorothy Fleming in 1775, but when seven years later she confessed to having entertained no fewer than twenty-seven lovers at Appuldurcombe House, Sir Richard brought a divorce action which created a national scandal. He gained his object, but the jury decided that he had 'encouraged this debauchery' and gave him only one shilling in compensation.

Wisely, Sir Richard decided to leave the country. He travelled abroad for five years, indulging his hobby of collecting works of art and classical antiquities, and Appuldurcombe House became a showcase for these items, more of a museum than a home. When Sir Richard died in 1805, the house passed to his niece, Henrietta, and the estate was sold in 1855.

Since 1909 Appuldurcombe House has been unoccupied, but recent restoration work and an informative exhibition help to recall the past grandeur of this magnificent mansion.

ISLE OF WIGHT
½ mile (0.8km) west of Wroxall off B3327 OS map 196: ref SZ 543800 Open year round; entrance fee payable Wheelchair access; car park ¼ mile (0.4km) from house Tel: Site office (0983) 852484

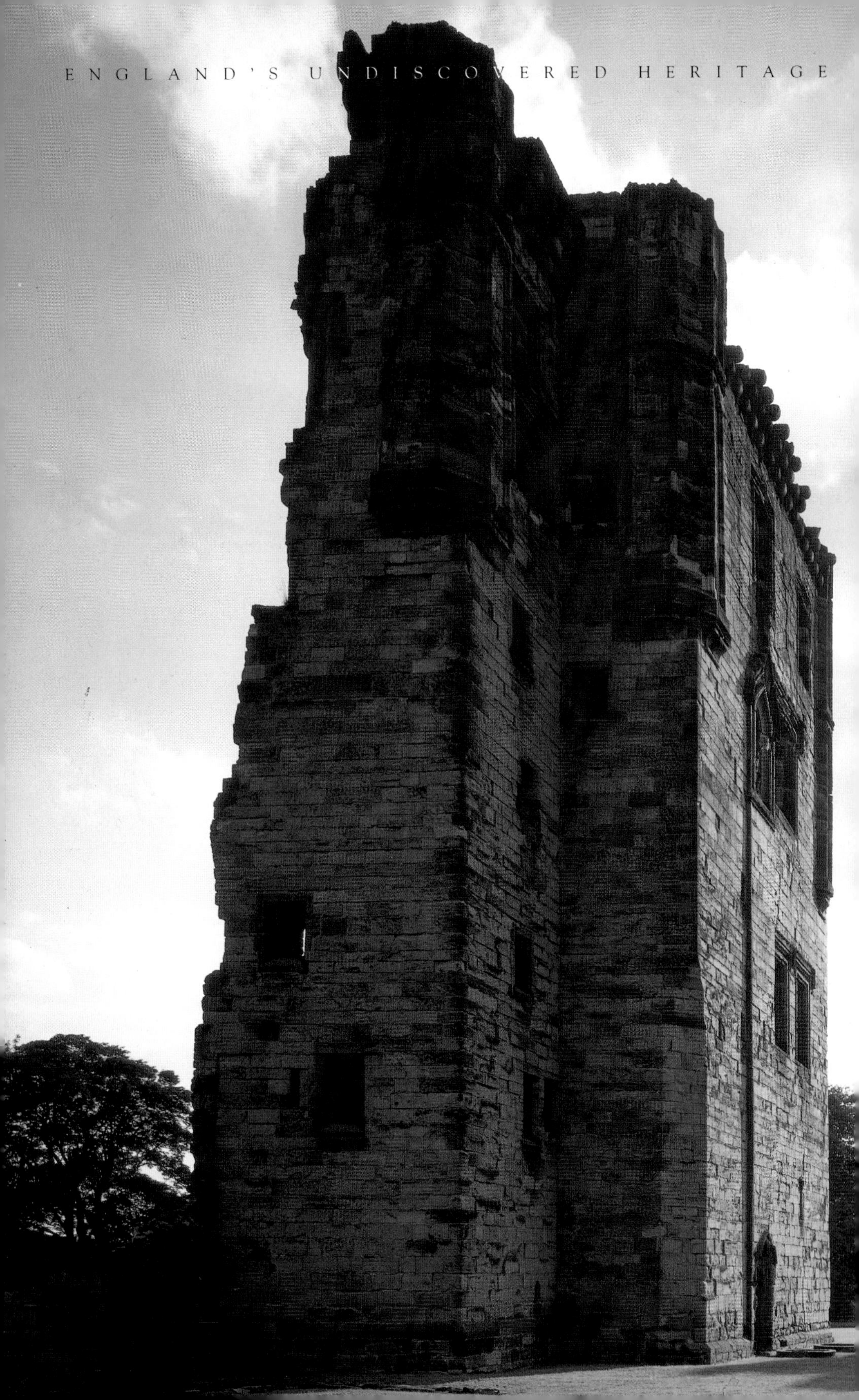

ASHBY DE LA ZOUCH CASTLE

Take a good torch and a pair of flat shoes when you visit Ashby de la Zouch Castle. You will need the torch for creeping along the passageway linking the kitchen with the Hastings Tower; and sensible shoes are a must for climbing the steep and narrow spiral staircase of the tower.

The castle, which developed around an existing manor house, dominates the small town of Ashby de la Zouch, a popular spa in the nineteenth century, situated on the edge of what was once the densely wooded Charnwood Forest. The earliest remains (sections of the walls in the hall, pantry and buttery) are from the mid-twelfth century. It was then that the manor passed to the Breton la Zouch family, who lived there until 1339.

Ownership of the manor was unsettled until 1464, when it was granted by Edward IV to his Lord Chamberlain William, Lord Hastings, who built both the elaborate tower on the perimeter wall and the unusually large chapel. (The east window of the nearby parish church of St Helen's contains the ancient heraldic glass from the chapel.) Only half of the Hastings Tower remains today. The entrance is on the north wall — a narrow doorway with rich mouldings around the archway — and immediately to the left is an uneven stone staircase leading to the upper floors. From the tiny windows of the stairwell there are views over what is now known as 'the wilderness', but was once a castle garden complete with bowling green and ornamental ponds. The tower was built for both accomodation and defence and the thick walls on the ground floor measure 8ft 7in (2.6m). It originally stood 90ft (27.4m) high, but now, having lost its parapet, battlements and angle turrets, it reaches about 75ft (22.8m).

Lord Hastings did not enjoy the fruits of his labour for long: he was beheaded by Richard III in 1483. But his descendants entertained royal visitors, including Henry VII, James I and Charles I. During the Civil War, under Henry Hastings, the castle became a centre of royalist operations. The defensive Mount House was built and

underground passages were dug for use in the event of a siege. Hastings was forced to surrender to the Roundheads in February 1646. Oliver Cromwell apparently came to survey the castle at about that time and took a drink at the Bull's Head, the fourteenth-century inn which still stands in the centre of the town.

The Ashby de la Zouch Museum has exhibits on the history of the castle and the Hastings family.

LEICESTERSHIRE

In Ashby de la Zouch, 17 miles (27.2km) northwest of
   Leicester on A50
OS map 128: ref SK 363167
Open year round; entrance fee payable
Wheelchair access to grounds only
Tel: Site office (05301) 413343

Ashby de la Zouch Museum*
13-15 Lower Church Street, Ashby de la Zouch
Open Easter to September; entrance fee payable
Tel: (0530) 415603

AYDON CASTLE

Aydon Castle, standing almost as it did in the Middle Ages, is one of the finest surviving manor houses in England. Restoration work, aided by the fact that there had been only minimal changes down the years, has been thorough and it is difficult to believe that tenant farmers actually lived here, albeit in damp conditions, until 1966.

The castle was built as a manor house in the late thirteenth-century by Robert de Reymes, the son of a wealthy Suffolk merchant. At the time, life on the Borders was relatively peaceful and Aydon had no defences. Hostilities between England and Scotland soon broke out, however, and by 1315 Reymes had been forced to build the circle of defensive walls which still stand on three sides of the castle. Aydon Castle was captured by the Scots in 1315 and by English rebels two years later. Long periods of non-resident and impoverished owners followed until the castle's conversion into a farmhouse in the seventeenth-century.

Today, visitors can step back to the time of Edward I and Edward II, when the castle was the home of a minor baron. The hall, chambers and service rooms, the servants' accommodation and the orchard outside can be viewed and are the subjects of interpretive display panels. The magnificent built-in fireplaces are a special point of interest.

The castle is set in a secluded spot overlooking the steep valley of Cor Burn, and the best view of it is from the footpath which follows a 2 mile (3.2km) scenic route to Corbridge.

NORTHUMBERLAND
1 mile (1.6km) northeast of Corbridge, on minor road off B6321 or A68 OS map 87: ref NZ 002663 Open summer months; entrance fee payable Wheelchair access to ground floor only Tel: Site office (043471) 2450

BACONSTHORPE CASTLE

The remains of Baconsthorpe Castle, notably the two flint-faced gatehouses and parts of the original curtain wall, indicate that it was once a handsome building. The castle, essentially a moated and fortified manor house, was begun in the 1480s by Sir John Heydon, a harsh and cunning lawyer who made his money during the Wars of the Roses. It was expanded and altered through the years by later members of the family and reflects their changing fortunes. The period that left the greatest mark on the castle buildings was the seventeenth century, when Baconsthorpe became the centre of a vast sheep run. The castle was transformed to house a wool industry.

The outer gatehouse is probably the most impressive part of the castle ruins. Built for show rather than defence, in Elizabethan times, this pretty Gothic-style gatehouse was lived in until 1920, when one of its two turrets collapsed. The castle courtyard owes its survival to the fact that it was used as the walled garden of the house.

NORFOLK
¾ mile (1.2km) north of village of Baconsthorpe off unclassified road 3 miles (4.8km) east of Holt
OS map 133: ref TG 122382
Open year round, entrance free
Tel: Area office (0223) 358911

BARNARD CASTLE

Dramatically situated above the river Tees, with sheer cliffs on two sides, Barnard Castle was once the largest castle in northern England and its ruins till evoke the strength of this powerfully positioned fortress. The site is both historic and picturesque.

Barnard Castle was built in the late eleventh century by Guy of Bailleul, a knight of Picardy, as a small earthwork castle. Thirty years later his nephew, Bernard de Baliol, began to create a large stone fortress on the site and it was he who gave his name to both the castle and the town. The castle remained in the Baliol family until 1296, when John Baliol, crowned King of Scotland in 1292, was defeated by Edward I. Ownership passed to the

Earls of Warwick, who held it for nearly two centuries. The castle then changed hands many times before being partially demolished in 1630. Its only real claim to military fame is that in 1569 the queen's steward held out bravely for eleven days against the Earls of Westmoreland and Northumberland, thus playing a vital part in quashing the 'Rising of the North'.

The castle's surviving remains date chiefly from the hundred years between 1250 and 1350. Apart from the curtain wall and the gatehouse, which are in the Town Ward, they are concentrated in the Inner Ward, the stronghold and place of residence, and are dominated by the tall Baliol, or Round, Tower, 36ft (11m) in diameter and 40ft

(12.1m) high, which served as the private quarters of the lords of Barnard Castle. The tower offers a lovely view, which was an inspiration for Sir Walter Scott when he was writing *Rokeby*. In the nineteenth century it was the home of a hermit, who lived at the top and grew vegetables in the ground below. His ghost is said to roam the ruins.

DURHAM

In Barnard Castle
OS map 92: ref NZ 049165
Open year round, part week only during winter months;
   entrance fee payable
Wheelchair access
Tel: Site office (0833) 38212

BELSAY HALL, CASTLE AND GARDENS

The Belsay estate, with its neo-classical
nineteenth-century hall, medieval castle,
Jacobean manor house and landscaped grounds, is
of great historic and architectural interest. It also
provides an insight into the changing way of life
on the Borders for one family, the Middletons,
who lived there from the time that the castle was
built c. 1370 until recent years.

The castle, an imposing tower-house built at a
time of great unrest, is recognized as a fine example
of strong fortification combined with spacious,
even luxurious, accommodation for the lord of the
manor. It stands three storeys high, with
battlements and parapets at roof level and small
circular towers at the four corners. The impressive
L-shaped tower rises above the battlements in the
southwest corner.

The manor house, void of any defences, was
built shortly after the union of the Scottish and
English crowns under James I (James VI of
Scotland) in 1603, and reflects the anticipation in
the Borders of greater security and a more peaceful
future. Indeed, it is one of the first unfortified
manor houses in the country. Proof of its date lies
in an inscription above the porch on the main
front of the house, which reads, 'Thomas
Middleton and Dorothy his wife builded this
House *anno* 1614'. Little now remains of the
manor house, and most of what does is from the
nineteenth century, but engravings and records
are on show to help create a picture of how it
looked originally.

The third stage of building at Belsay came in the
early nineteenth century, when the adventurous
Sir Charles Monck (who had changed his name
from Middleton in 1799) undertook a radical
development of the estate. Belsay Hall, completed
in 1815, was his personal triumph. A talented
draftsman with a keen eye for architectural detail,
Sir Charles made plans for this neo-classical
house, one of the most important in Britain, while
honeymooning on the Continent, where he
enjoyed both the German neo-classical style
which was becoming popular in Berlin and the
classical Greek architecture of Athens. During his
two years abroad he drew more than 200 plans and
sketches for Belsay Hall and on his return he
employed John Dobson, a local architect, to put
his ideas into practice. What makes this building
so outstanding, both externally and internally, is
the perfection of its proportions and the
painstaking attention to detail.

The hall is built of warm brown stone taken
from a quarry to the southwest of the house. Sir
Charles later made gardens in this and other
quarries on the estate, including in them many

rare and exotic plants which he had collected on
his travels. The quarry gardens are now a
mysterious mixture of light and dark, splashes of
colour against unfinished stone. They occupy,
however, only part of the magnificent grounds
designed by Sir Charles and his successors. The
grounds also include a rose garden, a winter
garden, a rhododendron garden, a woodland
garden and a meadow garden full of wild flowers.

NORTHUMBERLAND

14 miles (22.4km) northwest of Newcastle on A696
OS map 88: ref NZ 088785
Open during summer months; entrance fee payable
Wheelchair access to grounds only
Tel: Site office (066181) 636

BERKHAMSTED CASTLE

Little now remains of this Norman castle except its impressive earthworks. With the stonework in ruins, the earthworks give an extremely clear outline of the original motte and bailey dating back to the time of William the Conquerer.

The motte, a circular earthen mound, stands about 45ft (13.7m) high on a base 180ft (54.8m) in diameter. On its flattened summit there are remains of the keep and a well, reminders of the days when this was the lord of the manor's dwelling place and last line of defence. Stretching away from the motte is the oblong bailey, 450ft (137m) by 300ft (91.4m), which provided both the outer defence and space for a hall, stables, store-rooms, a chapel and a kitchen. The top of the motte offers a good view of the bailey and the surrounding double moat.

Berkhamsted Castle was one of the fortresses built by William the Conquerer across the country to secure his position as King of England and it occupied a special place in his grand plan. It was at Berkhamsted that the English surrendered to him in 1066 and, realizing the value of its strategic position, William gave the site to his half-brother, Robert, Count of Mortain. Set high on the northern slope of the valley of the river Bulborne, within a short distance from London, the castle became one of the most important in the country and a favourite royal residence until the time of Queen Elizabeth I. Among its many notable owners were Thomas Becket, who rented out the land for farming during his time as Lord Chancellor and Archbishop of Canterbury, and Edward the Black Prince, who spent his dying days here.

HERTFORDSHIRE

Adjacent to Berkhamsted station
OS map 165: ref SP 996083
Open year round, entrance free
Wheelchair access
Tel: Area office (01) 211 8828

BERWICK-UPON-TWEED FORTIFICATIONS

The most northerly town in England, Berwick was contested for three centuries by the English and Scots, changing hands at least thirteen times until it was eventually established as part of England in 1482. Its position naturally gave rise to extensive fortifications and Berwick is now recognized as one of the most outstanding fortified towns in Europe. The Elizabethan ramparts which encircle the town form one of the most complete artillery defences anywhere. A walking tour of the fortifications offers not only fascinating historical features, but also constantly changing and quite spectacular views of the river, sea, countryside and town. A good starting point is Scotsgate, the main entrance to the town from the north, followed by a circuit of the ramparts, taking slight detours to include the castle, the remains of the medieval town walls and the Ravensdowne Barracks.

Work began on the town walls in 1297, after Berwick was captured by Edward I. Edward rebuilt and strengthened the existing wooden defences and completely replanned the streets. Remains of these medieval walls can still be seen, especially around the Bell Tower, a watch-post for viewing the enemy, but for the most part they were replaced and repaired on the orders of Elizabeth I between 1558 and 1570. An Italian design was followed, intended to allow the most effective use of artillery. Low, thick earthworks faced with stone were broken at intervals by strongholds, or bastions, which ensured that every part of the walls was covered by gunfire. A 200ft (70m) wide ditch originally ran in front of the walls. The Elizabethan ramparts are in a remarkably good state of repair and you can walk along the top of the walls to explore the bastions, including Meg's Mount, Cumberland Bastion, Brass Bastion and King's Mount.

The first barracks were built in Berwick in 1717-1721 to replace the old system of billeting soldiers on the town's inhabitants. They were designed in the style of Vanburgh; the gateway is decorated with the arms of George I. The barracks were one of the first in Great Britain to be purpose-built, providing accommodation for officers, men and their families. They have changed little in appearance since the eighteenth-century, although they now house three museums: 'By Beat of Drum', a permanent exhibition tracing the life of the common soldier from the 1660s to the 1880s; the Museum of the King's Own Scottish Borders, who have had their headquarters here since 1881; and the Berwick Town Museum and Art Gallery.

Little remains of the ancient thirteenth-century castle. The railway station now occupies the site

and much of the original castle stone was used to build the railway bridge. Still visible, however, is the west wall, or White Wall as it is known, which now acts as a boundary for the railway yard but once guarded a flight of steps up the steep bank. A sixteenth-century gun tower on the river bank also survives.

NORTHUMBERLAND

Berwick Barracks
On the Parade, off Church Street, Berwick town centre
OS map 75: ref NT 994535
Open during summer months; entrance fee payable
Tel: Site office (0289) 304493

Berwick-Upon-Tweed Castle
Adjacent to Berwick railway station west of town centre
OS map 75: ref NT 994535
Open year round, entrance free

Berwick-Upon-Tweed Ramparts
Surrounding Berwick town centre on north bank of river Tweed
OS map 75: ref NT 994535
Open year round; guided tours in midsummer; entrance free
Wheelchair access
Tel: Area office (0228) 31777

BINHAM PRIORY

The magnificent west front of the priory church is the first thing that strikes visitors, a rich and elaborate example of Early English architecture. The great west window has been bricked up since 1809, but the bar tracery is admirable.

The priory itself was founded in the late eleventh century by Pierre de Valoines, nephew of William the Conqueror, as one of the eight cells of the Benedictine Abbey of St Albans. It had an eventful history under a series of unscrupulous, scheming and often scandalous priors, and suffered a siege c.1212, when the brethren had to eat bread made with bran and drink water from the rain-pipe. The priory surrendered to Henry VIII's dissolution of the monasteries in 1540. The monastic buildings were mostly pulled down, the stone being used for other buildings, but the nave of the church continued in use as the parish church. Today the Priory Church of St Mary and the Holy Cross, which is to some extent a ruin within a greater ruin, is an inspiring and unique place of worship, especially in the summer months when services are held at the open-air altar.

To the south of the church are the remains of the monastic area. Visitors enter through a precinct between the church and the cloister into the monk's outer parlour. Enough remains to give a good impression of the layout of the main buildings. It is possible to identify the chapterhouse, the warming room with hearth, the refectory (with the position of the pulpit for the reader during mealtimes), the reredorter, or latrines, the cellarer's range and the kitchens.

A medieval wayside cross stands on the village green at Binham, an additional interesting feature to be included in a visit to the priory.

NORFOLK

¼ mile (0.4km) northwest of village of Binham on Wells road off B1388
OS map 132: ref TF 982399
Open year round; entrance free
Tel: Area office (0223) 358911

Binham Wayside Cross
On village green at Binham
OS map 132: ref TF 986396

BISHOP'S WALTHAM PALACE

Bishop's Waltham Palace is a picturesque site to visit. A stunning view of the palace's tower, set off by a large copper beech tree, can be seen from the nearby country lane. Inside the grounds, there are many more beautiful trees, along with areas of wild flowers and carefully manicured lawns. The extensive remains of the palace are just a fragment of what was once one of the greatest residences of the richest bishopric of medieval England, that of Winchester. The land was acquired from King Edward the Elder in 1904 and may have been the seat of early Saxon bishops, but no definite evidence of a residence of importance survives from before the twelfth century.

During the thirteenth and fourteenth centuries, the palace continued to grow. Accounts show that the construction work was often carried out by leading craftsmen of the day. Work was done by Hugh Heland, one of the foremost carpenters, who is best known for the great roof of Westminster Hall; and the window glass was made by Thomas the Glasyer of Oxford, who also produced the glass for Winchester College. Flint for construction was collected locally, and timber was cut from neighbouring woods.

The palace survived the dissolution of the monasteries and continued to prosper until the Civil War. The bishop of the day supported King Charles and the palace became a royalist garrison. When the garrison was forced to surrender, there was terrible destruction: a contemporary report records that Bishop's Waltham was 'left in ashes'. Though never restored as a residence of bishops, the ruins remained in their ownership until 1869.

Apart from the ruins of the fortified palace, visitors today can also see a range of lodgings built during the mid-fifteenth century and adapted in the seventeenth century to form a farmhouse.

HAMPSHIRE
In Bishop's Waltham off B3035 or B2177
OS map 185: ref SU 552173
Open year round; part week only during winter; entrance fee payable
Wheelchair access to grounds only
Tel: Site office (04983) 2460

BLACKFRIARS

Blackfriars presents a record of continual unsympathetic alterations: modifications and additions can be seen dating from each century since its original construction. It was built in the mid-thirteenth century under the benefaction of Henry III, who provided timber for the roofs (much of which remains today). The royal accounts show that the oak came not only from the nearby Forest of Dean, but also from much further afield in Shropshire and Dorset. At its peak, Blackfriars accommodated between thirty and forty friars, but by the time of the dissolution of the monasteries numbers had dwindled to just seven. The friary was bought by Alderman Thomas Bell, three times mayor and sheriff of Gloucester, who made drastic changes in converting the buildings for manufacturing use. Much medieval work nevertheless survived, of which the south cloistral range is exemplary. From the road, Blackfriars has the appearance of a sixteenth-century mansion, but inside much is revealed of its origins.

GLOUCESTERSHIRE

In Gloucester, in Ladybellgate Street off Southgate Street and Blackfriars Walk
OS map 162: ref SO 830186
Open part week during summer season; entrance fee payable
Wheelchair access to ground floors only; assistance required
Tel: Site office (0452) 27688

BOLSOVER CASTLE

It certainly looks like a castle, with its battlements and turrets, but Bolsover is a fantastic folly built in the seventeenth century, the romantic whim of Sir Charles Cavendish and his son, William. It stands on the site of a Norman castle, but nothing remains of the original castle, which was demolished by Sir Charles to make way for his extraordinary mansion.

The present buildings were designed by Robert and John Smythson and work on them took place between c. 1608 and 1640. The oldest is the Little Castle, with the Fountain Garden leading from it that was probably meant to represent a keep and outer bailey. The exuberance of the exterior of the Little Castle is continued inside: twenty-six rooms are open to the public and although they are small, the decoration, especially of the Star Chamber and Heaven Chamber, is rich and colourful, with allegorical paintings, vaulted ceilings and elaborate carved fireplaces.

Stretching from the Little Castle on the west side of the Great Court is the Long Terrace Range, now roofless. This contains the major part of the

accommodation: a great banqueting hall and a State suite for reception of important guests, and rooms for family use. Forming the third side of the Great Court are the riding school, forge and stables. Built by William Cavendish, 'Horsemanship' Duke of Newcastle, during the 1630s, the riding school was one of the earliest of its kind in England. A window in the first-floor gallery overlooks the riding school (which is still in use) and gives a good view of the magnificent ornamental timber roof. An exhibition in the gallery gives a full history of the riding school and displays in the Little Castle explain more about the Cavendish family and the imaginative mansion.

DERBYSHIRE

In Bolsover, 6 miles (9.6km) east of Chesterfield on A362
OS map 120: ref SK 471707
Open year round; entrance fee payable
Wheelchair access except to castle keep
Tel: Site office (0246) 823349

BOSCOBEL HOUSE

Many people know that Charles Stuart, crowned king in Scotland and claiming to be King of England, hid in an oak tree after his defeat at the Battle of Worcester in 1651. Fewer people realize that the exact site of this famous tree is known, and that a descendant of it can be seen today near Boscobel House. The house itself, an attractive timber-framed building, also sheltered Charles during his escape. A small, secret room in the attic reached through a trapdoor at the top of the staircase is thought to have been his hiding place from 5-7 September, 1651.

Boscobel House was then a hunting lodge surrounded by dense forest, but in the late seventeenth century it was incorporated into a farmhouse, and the site is now set amid fertile fields. Apart from the famous oak tree and the attic, there is much to see — a guided tour offers visitors the history and legends to the house, and the lovely gardens are an additional pleasure.

The twelfth-century White Ladies' Priory, a short walk from Boscobel, shares this particular piece of history. It was to this nunnery that Charles came first on the evening after the battle.

SHROPSHIRE

On unclassified road between A41 and A5, 8 miles (12.8km) northwest of Wolverhampton
OS map 127: ref SJ 837083
Open year round; entrance fee payable
Wheelchair access to gardens only
Tel: Site office (0902) 850224

BRINKBURN PRIORY

The priory was founded, by William Bertram, c.1135 as a house for Augustinian canons. Only fragments of the cloister buildings remain, but the beautiful Romanesque church, one of the finest in the country, is still standing. It was built in 1190 and reroofed and restored in 1858. Noteworthy features are the lancet windows, glazed with stained glass, and the stone-vaulted roof. The organ, built in 1868 by the celebrated English organ-builder William Hill, is still intact and is occasionally used for recitals. Entrance to the church is by an elaborate north doorway, and one of the best views of this north portal is seen from the top of the steep path in the car park. The pathway provides a short walk through wild woodland to an almost secret opening which leads to the church and priory.

Perfectly secluded and peaceful, the site of Brinkburn Priory has a magical atmosphere. Tradition has it that nearby is the burial place for Northumbrian fairies, who loved the many wild flowers that grow around this picturesque and well-hidden spot in a loop of the River Coquet.

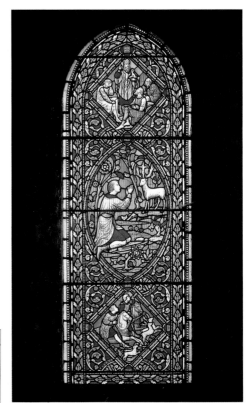

NORTHUMBERLAND

4½ miles (7.2km) southeast of Rothbury on unclassified road off B6334
OS map 81: ref NZ 116984
Open during summer months; entrance fee payable
Tel: Site office (066570) 628

BROUGH CASTLE

From the top of Brough Castle's Norman keep (up a narrow and seemingly endless spiral staircase) there are views, on a clear day, right down the valley, across the open moors and over the hills of the Lake District. The keep also provides a bird's-eye view of the castle's plan. The ruined three-storey gatehouse is from the early thirteenth century. Within the walls the kitchen can be identified in the northeast corner; it is known as Lady Anne's kitchen, after Lady Anne Clifford, who was responsible for restoration of the castle during the seventeenth century.

Brough was built over the site of a Roman fort known as Verterae, one of a number of fortifications which guarded the road from York via the Pennines to Carlisle. It had a turbulent history marked by many battles. A seige during the twelfth century was described by a contemporary observer, Jordan de la Fontaine:

> A new knight had come to them that day.
> Now hear of his deeds and great virtues.
> When all his companions had surrendered.
> He stayed in the keep and seized two shields,
> Which he hung on the battlements, where he stayed long.
> He threw at the Scots three sharp javelins;
> With each he struck a man dead.
> Then he took sharp stakes
> And hurled them at the Scots,
> Evermore shouting, 'You shall all be vanquished'.
> When the fire robbed him of the defence of the shields
> He was not to blame that he surrendered.
> Now is Brough overthrown and the better part of the tower.

CUMBRIA

8 miles (12.8km) southeast of Appleby, south of A66   OS map 91: ref NY 791141
Open year round, part week only during winter; entrance fee payable
Tel: Area office (0228) 31777

BROUGHAM CASTLE

The name Brougham is a corruption of the Celtic word *brocavum*, which means 'home of the badgers'. It was the name adopted by the Romans for their powerful fortress on this site. Brocavum commanded an important crossing point over the river Eamont and it quickly became a major road junction. The western road from Scotland was joined by a trunk road which ran along the Eden Valley and over the Pennines to York. Such a strategically important fortress, housing about 1000 troops, attracted numerous traders and a settlement, or *vicus*, soon developed around it. Recent aerial photographs indicate that there was substantial farming activity.

Brougham's next important historic development took place in the early thirteenth century when Robert de Vipont built a keep on the Roman site. Later in the century Roger, first Lord Clifford, built a considerable defensive complex around the keep. During the fourteenth century the fifth Lord Clifford changed the layout of the castle, built a chapel, and added a number of finishing touches. Above the gatehouse arch may be seen the inscription 'this made Roger'.

In the seventeenth century Lady Anne Clifford restored the castle as an ancestral seat (she died here in 1676). Proud of her long ancestry, she lived a grand life, travelling around her various castles with a court of attendants and servants. But she was also a prudent property manager who kept careful note of her expenditures. An entry in her account book for October 1673 reads:

Pay'd to Richard Lowes my Housekeeper at Brougham Castle for board and wages for 10 weeks at 2:6 per week 30s [sic]; and for keeping his catt at that time 3d per week 2:6.

Today's visitor can admire the Tudor details added to Brougham by Lady Anne and study the ruins which reveal much of the castle's history. The surrounding area is also worth exploring. The ancient church of St Wilfred's repays a visit and nearby there are two huge henges, both some 4000 years old. To the southeast is the Countess Pillar, set up by Lady Anne in 1656 and thought to have been the impost of a Roman arch from Brocavum. On three sides there are sundials and on the fourth a bronze inscription explains that the pillar commemorates the spot where Lady Anne parted from her mother for the last time in 1616.

CUMBRIA

1½ miles (2.4km) southeast of Penrith
OS map 90: ref NY 537290
Open year round, part week only during winter; entrance fee payable
Wheelchair access except to castle keep
Tel: Site office (0768) 62488

Countess Pillar
1 mile (1.6km) southeast of Brougham on A66
Open year round; entrance free

BUILDWAS ABBEY

Situated on the banks of the river Severn (the abbey derived some of its income from tolls paid for river crossings), Buildwas Abbey is an attractive place to visit. The bluntly pointed arches of the church nave, which frame the surrounding countryside, are a dramatic landmark and on a lower ground level, the cloister offers much to discover. A doorway in the east range leads into the crypt, the ceiling of which is a three-bayed groin vault. The chapterhouse contains some interesting lead-glazed tiles depicting animals and birds; these are purely decorative and are thought to date from the time of the abbey's construction, c.1200. The floor of the nave and the transepts may once have been covered with such tiles, and it's interesting to note that the abbey stands in a part of the county of Shropshire which later, during the nineteenth century, became a world leader in tile manufacture.

Life at the abbey was mostly uneventful, though it did have some colourful and even dangerous incidents. In 1342 a renegade monk, Thomas Tong, murdered the abbot, or so it was alleged. In 1350, a succeeding abbot was kidnapped by marauders from Wales: plundering by the Welsh was relatively common, and the practice became known as 'the levity of the Welsh'.

SHROPSHIRE
On south bank of river Severn on unclassified road off B4378 2 miles (3.2km) west of Iron Bridge OS map 127: ref SJ 642044 Open year round; entrance fee payable Wheelchair access Tel: Site office (095245) 3274

BURTON AGNES OLD MANOR HOUSE

The Old Manor House is dwarfed by the splendid formal facade of Burton Agnes Hall, in the shadow of which it stands. The hall, built between 1601 and 1611, is still inhabited, but some of the rooms are open to the public between spring and autumn. The hall retains its Tudor and Jacobean decoration and possibly its ghost, Ann Griffith. Known in the local village as 'odd Nance', Anne is said to walk around the hall before disappearing into the painting known as 'The Ravencroft Boys'. Do ask about the story of her skull; it's a very strange tale indeed.

The Old Manor has no resident spirit, but it does have an interesting and chequered history having been, at various times, a baronial hall, service quarters and even a laundry! Its lands were recorded in the Domesday Survey of 1086, when the site formed part of the estate confiscated by the Crown from the Earl of Morcar. The two-storey house is twelfth-century, built in a typical Norman style. The upper floor, reached by a narrow spiral staircase, was the main living area and the vaulted undercroft was probably used for storage. The lower part may also have provided sleeping quarters for servants (the game of Nine Men's Morris — one of the oldest games known in Great Britain — is marked out on one of the central columns).

Just behind the Old Manor House stands St Martin's Church — 'the church of the Dark Knights and Gospel Lights'. It is reached by an archway of yew which has sheltered its entrance for some 300 years (the yew, common in churchyards, is a symbol of immortality).

HUMBERSIDE

In Burton Agnes village, 5 miles (8km) southwest of Bridlington on A166
OS map 101: ref TA 103633
Open year round; entrance free
Wheelchair access
Tel: Area office (0904) 58626

BUSHMEAD PRIORY

In the heart of the Bedfordshire countryside, at the end of a leafy lane, stands what appears to be a private house. This was once the refectory hall of Bushmead Priory, a small Augustinian house founded c.1195, and it is all that now remains of it. Inside, the beautifully preserved timber-framed crown-post roof is quite magnificent, the priory's outstanding feature. Dating back to the mid-thirteenth century, it is one of the earliest surviving parts of the building. During the dissolution of the monasteries in 1537, the priory was bought by William Gery, a prosperous landed gentleman, who converted it into a family home. The family (who became the Wade-Gerys in 1792) lived in it until 1973 and made extensive alterations. There has been dedicated conservation work to the house, both externally and internally; the photographs on display show the work at its different stages.

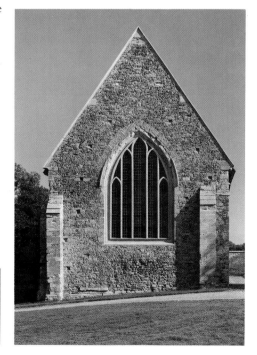

BEDFORDSHIRE

7 miles (11.2km) north of Bedford on unclassified road near Colmworth
OS map 153: ref TL 115607
Open during summer months; entrance fee payable
Tel: Site office (023062) 614

BYLAND ABBEY

When approached by road, Byland Abbey is not immediately visible: its stone walls seem to blend into the countryside, especially on an autumn day, amid the softened colours of the surrounding land and trees. Yet there is a substantial complex to explore. The most dramatic of the remains is the west front of the church which, when it was built in the twelfth-century, was a magnificent edifice worked to the highest standards of its day. Its cloister is some 145ft (44m) square, making it larger than those at Fountains Abbey and Rievaulx Abbey. The church was once almost totally paved with yellow and green glazed tiles, the spectacular effect of which can be imagined by looking at the floors of the two chapels in the south transept. Imagine, too, those colourful floors juxtaposed with whitewashed walls lined out with a masonry pattern in red. (The carved capitals were also picked out in red and examples can be seen in the small site museum.)

The best view of Byland's plan is from the corner of the site diametrically opposite the entrance kiosk. Here the land slopes gently upwards, providing an excellent panorama.

NORTH YORKSHIRE
2 miles (3.2km) south of A170 between Thirsk and Helmsley, near Coxwold village OS map 100: ref SE 549789 Open year round; entrance fee payable Wheelchair access Tel: Site office (03476) 614

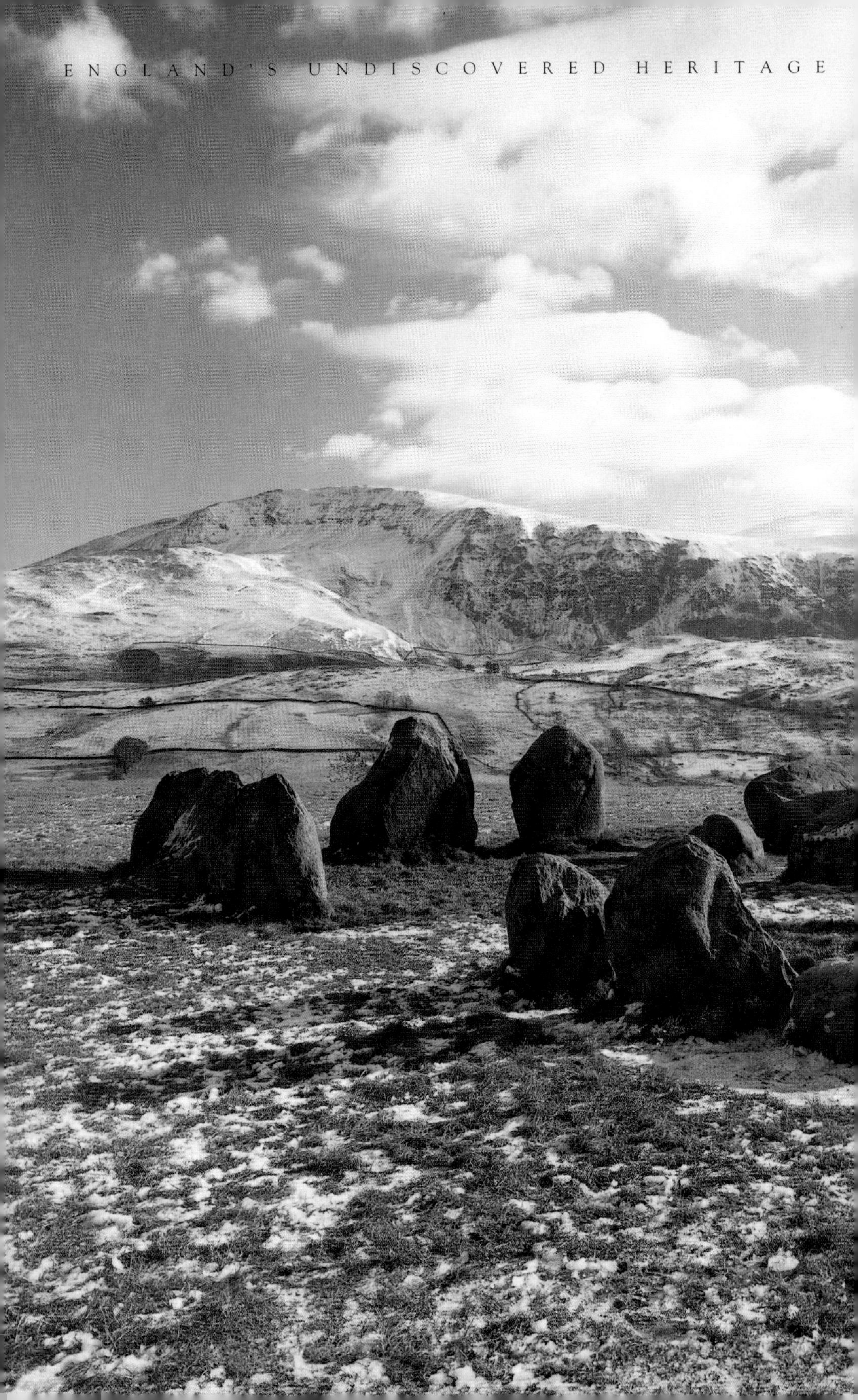

CASTLERIGG STONE CIRCLE

These ancient lichen-dappled stones glow a lurid lime green with the last cold rays of clear autumn sunshine. Autumn is, arguably, the best time to visit the Castlerigg stones, but at any time of year the scenery is breathtaking. The stone circle is situated on a small mound, surrounded by the mountains of the Lake District. Silent and majestic, they provide the perfect setting for this fascinating monument, which is known locally as the Druids' Circle, but which certainly predates the Druids. It was probably erected c. 1500BC, during the Bronze Age. Little is known of its origins. Large stone circles exist mainly on the west side of England and it is thought that they were religious meeting places. Despite excavations at Castlerigg during the last century, no evidence has been discovered to confirm that this was so.

CUMBRIA
1½ miles (2.4km) east of Keswick on unclassified road between A66 and A591 OS map 90: ref NY 293236 Open year round; entrance free Tel: Area office (0228) 31777

CASTLE RISING CASTLE

The strange name may lead you to expect that this castle is situated on particularly high ground, but the term 'rising' is of Saxon origin, thought to be a derivation from a personal name or a feature on the site, and nothing to do with the lie of the land. The strangeness is in the sight of the partially ruined Norman keep completely surrounded by huge and quite formidable grass ramparts and ditches. The keep is large, but appears smaller than it is because encircled by these impressive earthworks. A walk along the ramparts affords beautiful views of the surrounding countryside.

Entrance to the inner bailey is over a stone bridge and through a ruined Norman gatehouse. These are the only castle buildings other than the great keep to survive. The keep itself is entered via the forebuilding , the exterior of which bears traces of the original rich decoration and the remains of interlacing arches. Within the forebuilding is the main stairway, a splendid stone staircase leading to a warren of dimly lit rooms and galleries, roofless and floorless, but absolutely intriguing. Just north of the keep, the base of the walls of an ancient Norman church can be seen.

The castle was built c. 1140 as a dwelling for William d'Albini, Earl of Sussex, who was eager to display the new wealth he had acquired by marrying Queen Alice, widow of Henry I. One of the most important castles in East Anglia, it was granted to Thomas Howard, Duke of Norfolk, by Henry VIII in 1544, and remains in the ownership of the Howard family.

NORFOLK

4 miles (6.4km) northeast of King's Lynn off A149
OS map 132: ref TF 666246
Open year round; part week only in winter; entrance free
Tel: Site office (055387) 330

CLEEVE ABBEY

'Gate be open, shut to no honest person' — so runs the Latin inscription above the arch of the gateway to Cleeve Abbey, founded at the end of the twelfth century and inhabited by Cistercian monks until the monastery was dissolved in 1537. Known as the 'White Monks' because of the colour of their homespun habits, they devoted their lives to toil and prayer — farming the fields around them, tending their flocks of sheep and working on beautiful illumination of manuscripts.

Little remains of their abbey church. The east and south ranges are remarkably intact, but for the rest, only the low walls and foundations are to be seen. The plan of the church is still discernible — the quire for singing of the Office by the monks and the nave, where excavations revealed an abbot's stone coffin (still on show). The church, as was normal, stood to the north of the cloister. The rooms to the east of the cloister, known as the east range, are mainly thirteenth century. The south range or frater range, as it is often called, was remodelled in the fifteenth century, when Abbot David Juyner set about reviving the ailing fortunes of the monastery.

Among the rooms on the ground floor of the east range is the sacristy, with its rose window and painted decoration dating from the thirteenth century. On the floor is a mosaic made up of tiny fragments of tiles found during nineteenth-century excavations. In the common room are the remains of the fireplace — the fire would be lit on 1 November, the Feast of All Saints, and was kept burning until Easter. Occupying the whole of the

first floor of the east range is the dorter, one of the finest remaining examples of an early monastic dormitory in England. It was designed to accommodate thirty-six monks, although even at the height of Cleeve's prosperity there were only twenty-eight.

The south range is equally fascinating, especially the fifteenth-century frater, or dining hall, on the first floor. The workmanship of the timber roof is quite superb, and it is decorated with rows of carved angels. An almost hidden doorway at the top of the frater stairs leads to another impressive room, the painted chamber. The east wall is completely covered with a wall painting so detailed that you can pick out the different types of fish swimming in the river.

There are still remains of the original thirteenth-century frater on the ground floor of the south range, most notably the tile pavement which was once its floor. This was earthed over in the fifteenth century when the new frater was built, and not uncovered until four centuries later. The tiles are still very much in their original arrangement, divided into three main compartments, and visitors can become fascinated by study of the motifs and heraldry.

SOMERSET
In Washford, ¼ mile (0.4km) south of A39 OS map 181: ref ST 047407 Open year round; entrance fee payable Wheelchair access to grounds and ground floor only Tel: Area office (0272) 734472

DOVER CASTLE: THE ROMAN PHAROS AND CHURCH OF SAINT-MARY-IN-THE-CASTLE

Dover Castle, one of the largest and most important castles in England, is much-visited and well-documented, but within the castle grounds stands a less widely appreciated feature, a Roman pharos, or lighthouse, probably dating back to the first century AD. The lighthouse tower, octagonal on the outside and rectangular inside, was built in eight stages and stood nearly 230ft (24m) high. Only four stages remain today, the highest of which dates from rebuilding in the early fifteenth century; but several well-preserved Roman features, notably the entrance on the south side, are still visible.

After building of the Saxon church of St-Mary-in-the-Castle, which stands opposite, the pharos became a bell-tower, linked by an enclosed passage and west door. It continued to have this function until 1690, when the church ceased to be used and fell into disrepair. Now restored and back in use as the garrison church, St Mary is another little-known 'find' within the castle precinct. Although considerably altered and renovated over the years, it retains much original material, including Roman brick, re-used during the restoration work, and the Saxon south doorway. The stone beside the pulpit, inscribed with the Canterbury pilgrims' mark of three interconnecting circles, suggests that pilgrims stayed at Dover Castle on their way to Canterbury; although only persons of importance would have been accommodated here. Another stone, found during restoration work carried out in 1860, is part of the 'board' of Nine Men's Morris, a popular game throughout medieval England with a history dating back to ancient Egypt, where also it was a pastime of stonemasons.

KENT
On the east side of Dover
OS map 179: ref TR 326416
Open year round; entrance fee payable (entry to castle)
Wheelchair access to courtyards and grounds, assistance required
Tel: Site office (0304) 201628

EASBY ABBEY

The Abbey of St Agatha at Easby, founded *c*. 1155 and picturesquely positioned on the left bank of the River Swale, housed canons of the Premonstratensian order. This religious order, founded in 1120 at the Abbey of Prémontré, was introduced into England in 1143. The Premonstratensians followed a strict rule based upon the letter of St Augustine of Hippo:

0330 – rise	1200 – recreation hour
0400 – mattins	1300 – study
0530 – prime	1400 – vespers, study
0630 – breakfast	1700 – rosary
0700 – study	1730 – supper
0900 – terce, mass, study	1900 – compline
1100 – dinner	2030 – retire

Despite their rigid way of life, the canons of Easby Abbey were famed for their hospitality and

remains of the house, hall and solar used for guests still survive, as do the gatehouse, the infirmary, the abbot's lodgings and the frater, or refectory (which covers the whole of the south range). Part of the chapterhouse is still visible, together with the cloister and a small part of the church.

Nearby is Easby Parish Church (the churches of Mansfield and Easby belonged to the abbey). Its frescos, which date from the mid-thirteenth century, give a good idea of the dress and the habits of that age and are excellent examples of medieval church decoration.

NORTH YORKSHIRE
1 mile (1.6km) southeast of Richmond on unclassified road south of B6271
OS map 92: ref NZ 185003
Open year round; entrance fee payable
Tel: Area office (0904) 58626

EGGLESTONE ABBEY

Its charming pastoral setting beside the river Tees makes Egglestone Abbey a joy to visit. The abbey ruins offer beautiful views of the surrounding countryside, and from the abbey there are lovely walks to Barnard Castle. The abbey itself, one of the thirty-three houses of the Premonstratensian order in England and Wales, was founded c. 1198 by Ralph de Multon. It was never very important; on the contrary, its chief claim to fame was its poverty: in the fifteenth century a special inquiry was held to discuss whether the abbey should be reduced to the status of priory because it was so small and poor. Nor was the level of religious life very high; a report of 1502 noted many serious offences against the discipline of the order.

The abbey survived, precariously, until it was surrendered to Henry VIII in 1540. Eight years later the site was granted to Robert Strelly, who converted the domestic buildings and lived there.

Various occupants followed and over the years parts of the buildings were destroyed — not by neglect, nor by the elements, but by owners who took away spoils to use elsewhere. Much of the ashlar stone, for example, was removed to pave the stable yard of Rokeby Hall. Early in the twentieth-century fragments were returned and preserved, (such as the marble tomb of Sir Ralph Bowes of Streatlam, found in a neglected state in Mortham Wood) and although the abbey is far from complete, substantial sections of the cruciform church and cloistral buildings remain.

DURHAM
1 mile (1.6km) south of Barnard Castle on minor road off B6277 OS map 92: ref NZ 062151 Open year round; entrance free Wheelchair access Tel: Area office (0228) 31777

ELTHAM PALACE

Out in the suburbs of the busy capital city, amid a leafy enclave, can be found the remains of the once-fine palace of Eltham. It was described in a survey of royal estates carried out by parliament in 1649 as 'a Capital Mansion House built with brick, stone and timber and consisting of one fair chapel, one great hall, thirty-six rooms and offices below stairs with two large cellars, and above stairs in lodgings, called the King's side seventeen, the Queen's side twelve, the Prince's side nine, in all thirty-eight lodging rooms with other necessary rooms and closets.' Much has since been lost, but the great hall (recently restored) has withstood centuries of challenge. Its hammer-beam roof is dramatic, and so are the double-height oriels. Outside are the ruined remains of some the lodgings, but perhaps more significant is the bridge built by Richard II, which spans a water-filled moat.

Study any modern map of the area around Eltham Palace and you will quickly spot roads and lanes which have royal associations – King's Orchard, Prince John Road, Court Yard, Tiltyard Approach, Archery Yard. Almost every monarch from Henry III to Charles I visited the palace. One tradition — by no means reliable — has it that the Order of the Garter was established during a royal tournament at Eltham in 1347. Plenty of commoners are associated with Eltham too, including the poet Chaucer, who was clerk of the works for the palace and is said to have lost £20 (a huge sum for the time) while visiting.

Running down from the palace is King John's Walk, which passes between the moat and the attractive half-timbered Chancellors's lodgings (which can be viewed only from the exterior) and leads eventually to a meadow with a panoramic view over south London.

LONDON

Off A208, ¼ mile (0.4km) south from A210 (Court Yard, SE9)
   or ¾ mile (1.2km) north from A20 (Court Road, SE9)
Open year round, part week only; entrance free
Wheelchair access
Tel: Army Education Corps (01) 859 2112

FARLEIGH HUNGERFORD CASTLE

If the ruins of Farleigh Hungerford Castle promise a fascinating visit, so too do the terrible tales of the rich and unscrupulous Hungerford family, who lived here from 1370 to 1686. There is the story of Agnes, widow of Sir Edward Hungerford who was hanged at Tyburn in 1523, who is alleged to have ordered two men to strangle her former husband, John Cotell, at Farleigh Castle and burn his body in the kitchen furnace. And there was Walter, Lord Hungerford of Heytesbury, who was executed in 1540 for treason and unnatural vice, and whose third wife wrote to Thomas Cromwell complaining that she had been kept prisoner in one of the towers of the castle for three or four years, with food and drink deliberately rationed to her. The catalogue of crimes associated with Farleigh Hungerford is long and curious.

The castle was essentially a manor house, strengthened and fortified after 1383 by Sir Thomas de Hungerford, who was the first acknowledged Speaker of the House of Commons. It is now in almost total ruin, though the chapel is still standing and the priest's house has been rebuilt with some of the original features intact. The chapel, originally the Parish Church of St Leonard, dates form the mid-fourteenth century and contains a remarkable collection of tombs, including that of Sir Thomas, the builder of the castle. Perhaps the finest of the tombs is that of Sir Edward Hungerford, who died in 1648, and his wife, Margaret Holliday: the marble tomb effigies show some superb detailing. Beneath the chapel is the crypt, dark, dank and somewhat eerie, and containing the leaden coffins of three females, three males and two infants, none of whom have been identified. Near the entrance once stood a leaden urn, thought to have contained the embalmed heart of Sir Edward Hungerford; but it was stolen in 1822 and has never been returned.

The priest's house next to the church has now been converted into an exhibition space showing the history of the castle and the surrounding area. A notable exhibit is the Bible, dated 1611, known as the 'he bible' because of a printing error in Ruth III, 15. It is open at the appropriate page.

SOMERSET

In Farleigh Hungerford 3½ miles (5.6km) west of Trowbridge on A366
OS map 173: ref ST 801577
Open year round, part week only during winter months; entrance fee payable
Wheelchair access to exterior only
Tel: Area office (0272) 734472

FARNHAM CASTLE KEEP

The huge twelfth century keep of Farnham Castle is a most interesting structure. The motte is not on top of the mound, as was the norm, but was built at ground level and then surrounded by a conical mound. The castle was built c. 1138 by Bishop Henry of Blois, grandson of William the Conqueror and younger brother of King Stephen. The rectangular stone keep stood on top of the mound, but after the castle was damaged in 1155 and rebuilding put in hand some years later, the older keep was buried and replaced by a hollow shell keep. This is now in ruins: it was 'slighted' during the Civil War and the stones used to repave the town. Parts, however, have been well preserved and you can climb on top of the mound, where excavations have unearthed remains of the original Norman tower. From here there are good views of the other castle buildings.

The castle was the seat of the bishops of Winchester from the time of building until 1927 when it transferred to the bishops of Guildford, who retained it until 1955. The domestic buildings, largely from the thirteenth century, are now occupied by the Centre for International Briefing, but are open to the public for guided tours on a regular basis.

SURREY
½ mile (0.8km) north of Farnham town centre on A287 OS map 186: ref SU 839474 Open during summer months; entrance fee payable Tel: Site office (0252) 713393

FURNESS ABBEY

This red sandstone ruin is all that remains of what was once the wealthiest monastery in the Lake District and the second richest Cistercian house in England (Fountains Abbey was the richest). A medieval clerk wrote that the abbey was 'situated on a island', and certainly the site was once an inhospitable spot between the waters of Morecambe Bay, the undrained lands of southern Westmorland and the imposing hills of the Lake District. Yet despite, or perhaps because of, its isolation, the abbey suffered from being on what was then the frontier between England and Scotland. It also suffered, during the twelfth century, from raids mounted by an ex-monk, Widmund, who had turned pirate.

Furness Abbey evolved strong links with Ireland and the Isle of Man. A harbour was built at Piel to facilitate trading with the two islands and for a while, the abbot of Furness exercised the right to nominate the Bishop of Man. In Ireland the abbey had daughter houses in County Down (founded c.1187) and county Limerick (founded c.1206) and for a short time in the thirteenth century it controlled the houses of Corcomroe and Fermoy. A Furness monk, Jocelyn, wrote the lives of St Patrick and St Kentigern. The abbey's power was not, however, confined to the islands off Furness; its importance and established reputation during this period are attested to by the indulgences granted to it, not only by Irish and Manx bishops but also from bishoprics in England, Scotland and Wales. Royal officials visited the abbey and its original feudal privileges were gradually augmented. The abbey mined local deposits of iron and acquired extensive lands.

The abbey's peace, however, was continually disturbed by the Scots. In the early fourteenth century border warfare broke out and the lands around Furness were raided. The *Lanercost Chronicle* noted that the Scots 'laid waste everything as far as Furness . . . taking with them men and women as prisoners, especially were they delighted with the abundance of iron ore which they found there because Scotland is not rich in iron'. To save the abbey, the abbot went to meet the Scots leader, Robert Bruce, and paid him ransom for the district of Furness: and so the abbey survived. But several centuries later, despite favourable testimonies from the abbey's tenants (one Robert Wayles testified that every tenant with a plough was entitled to send two people to eat at the abbey once a week, and that children and labourers could go there for food and drink) the abbey and its possessions were passed over to the Crown.

Near Furness Abbey is another interesting feature of the area, the fifteenth century Bow Bridge. This ancient crossing of Mill Beck once connected Furness Abbey with medieval routes in the region. It was intended for pack-horse traffic and may originally have had stone parapets on each side.

CUMBRIA

1½ miles (2.4km) north of Barrow-in-Furness, on minor road off A590
OS map 96: ref SD 218717
Open year round; entrance fee payable
Wheelchair access
Tel: Site office (0229) 23420

Bow Bridge
Northeast of Barrow-in-Furness on minor road off A590 or A5087
OS map 96: ref SD 224 715
Open year round; entrance free

GAINSBOROUGH OLD HALL

One of the largest and most complete late medieval manor houses in England, Gainsborough Old Hall has had a varied and eventful history. It was built in the first half of the fifteenth-century by Sir Thomas Burgh, who had the distinction of surviving the reigns of four kings by allying himself always with the right side! Much of what remains today is from the late fifteenth-century — the hall was entirely rebuilt after being wrecked in 1470 by Lancastrian supporters in the Wars of the Roses — and there were considerable alterations made during the sixteenth century. While the Burgh family lived there, the Old Hall entertained many distinguished visitors, including Richard III, who stayed in 1483, and Henry VIII, who visited twice, first in 1509 and then again in 1540, when he was introduced to his last wife, Katharine Parr, widow of Sir Thomas's eldest son.

The house was sold to William Hickman, a London merchant, in 1597 and another chapter of history began. The family allowed members of the Separatist Church, the sect that was later to become the Mayflower Pilgrims, to meet here in the early seventeenth century. The Old Hall was sold in 1720 and since then it has been used as tenement dwellings, a linen factory, a soup kitchen, a ballroom, a corn exchange, a parish church, a theatre, an auction sale-room and even a Masonic lodge. Restoration work was begun in 1949 by a voluntary organization and the Lincolnshire County Council took possession of the building in 1979. The rooms are being renovated by English Heritage and furnished to show daily life during the house's somewhat erratic history.

The great hall, once the centre of the late medieval household, boasts a magnificant single-arch braced roof. It leads on to the medieval kitchen, little altered and now filled with figures, food and equipment showing the preparations for entertaining Richard III. Upstairs the solar room, which looks down on the great hall, contains a display on Richard III and the Burgh family. The tower houses a replica loom, a woolsack and information on the wool trade.

The upper great chamber and other rooms are haunted, so the story goes, by the sad and ghostly figure of 'The Lady in Grey' who roams the corridors looking for her long-lost knight.

LINCOLNSHIRE

In Gainsborough, opposite the libary
OS map 121: ref SK 815895
Open Easter to October; entrance fee payable
Wheelchair access to Great Hall only
Tel: Site office (0427) 2669

GOODRICH CASTLE

Looking at the high spur of land on which
Goodrich stands, it is easy to understand why
there has been a castle on this site for over 800
years. It commands excellent views across the
Wye valley, especially towards the ancient
crossing place on the river. On the opposite bank
of the river, the village of Walford (a corruption of
Welsh ford) dates from the time when the river
marked the boundary between Wales and
England. The surrounding hills provide an
impressive panorama around the castle, but it is
hardly dwarfed by its spectacular surroundings.

Goodrich Castle was largely the work of
William de Valence, half-brother to Henry II, but
its name derives from Godric — probably Godric
Mappestone who appears in a list of tenants. It is a
bold and strong fortress: high walls, massive
cylindrical towers which emerge from battered
square bases and a deep moat combine to make a
daunting approach to the castle. Yet inside the
protective outer 'skin', the architecture takes on a
gentler, more domestic air. The great hall on the
west side of the courtyard contains the remains of a
fireplace and a small vestibule above which is a
little chapel. The vestibule leads to private
chambers, including the solar room, which
features a screen of two arches springing from a
central pier and extending through two storeys.
The remains of the kitchen, found beside the
southwest tower, contain three ovens and a
fireplace.

Incorporated into the plan is the old Norman
keep, striking in its simplicity and of a mellow
green stone which contrasts with the vivid red of
the surrounding remains. Beside it is the entrance
to the castle dungeon, which usually provides a
great lure for children.

HEREFORD & WORCESTER
5 miles (8km) south of Ross-on-Wye off A40
OS map 162: ref SO 579199
Open year round; entrance fee payable
Tel: Site office (0600) 890538

GOODSHAW CHAPEL

A close look at the walls around Goodshaw Chapel reveals the traces of doors and windows belonging to old cottages which once clustered in the chapel's shadow. Goodshaw Chapel was built in 1760 by a congregation of Baptist worshippers, led by their minister, John Nettell. By 1860, the focus of community life had moved to the area around the new turnpike road (now the main road to Burnley) and when a new church was built, Goodshaw was deserted.

Today, visitors can see a well-preserved, authentic eighteenth-century Baptist chapel, restored to its original colours and furnished with fixtures and fittings which mostly date from around 1800. There is one section of pews — at the rear on the left — which is thought to be original. Underneath the wooden floor of each pew is a coffin, some forty-five in all, evidence that at one time there was a parliamentary ruling forbidding Nonconformists from being laid to rest in church burial grounds.

The atmosphere of the chapel is not at all funereal, however. Music played an important part in its activities and a group of local musicians known as the 'larks of Dean' were among those providing lively performances. The accoustics in Goodshaw Chapel are excellent.

Hundreds of coat pegs around the chapel walls suggest that the congregation was large, and Sunday School records of the early 1800s show some 300 or 400 children in attendance. During your visit, take the opportunity to stand in the pulpit and see what the minister would have seen — the seat of every single member of the congregation.

LANCASHIRE

2½ miles (4km) south of Burnley on minor road east of A56
OS map 103: ref SD 815263
Open year round, weekends by appointment; entrance free
Tel: Area office (0904) 58626

In MEMORY of
William Nutter, who died Oct 18th 1821
aged 62 Years.

An honest man, sincere, free from strife,
Who blameless past this vale of human life,
His worth approv'd beloved his upright mind,
Prepar'd for future bliss his breath resign'd.
True to the church, and constant to his God,
The pious christian's course he firmly trod.
Reader, his life contemplate for thy guide,
He liv'd respected, and lamented dy'd.

THE GRANGE, NORTHINGTON

Set amid glorious grounds, at the end of a long tree-lined lane, The Grange is one of the first and most important neo-classical country houses in England. Designed by William Wilkins, the architect of the National Gallery in London, it was built between 1809 and 1816 and takes the form of a Greek temple set around the core of a late seventeenth-century brick mansion.

The Grange was the idea of Henry Drummond, grandson of the famous banker of the same name. Drummond paid a small fortune to have his house remodelled in the fashionable Greek revival style. He soon lost interest, however, and in 1816 the house was sold to Alexander Baring, the banker and politician, who became the first Lord Ashburton in 1835. Lady Ashburton transformed the Grange into a popular meeting place for politicians and literary people: among the many guests were the writer Thomas Carlyle and his wife, Jane. Carlyle thought the house beautiful, but Jane complained that her bedroom made her feel 'ill at ease'. She described the Grange as a 'country house with a vengeance ... the inside is magnificent to death ... the ceilings all painted with fresco – some dozen rooms ... fitted up like rooms in an Arabian Night's entertainment.'

Although The Grange is now deserted and the interior gutted, Wilkins's exterior and the seventeenth-century west front have been restored. A site exhibition tells the story of The Grange and the personalities connected with it, including George IV, while he was Prince of Wales, who rented the house from 1795 to 1800. Although he claimed to be enjoying the estate for its well-stocked hunting, it is more likely that he chose this quiet, secluded spot as the ideal place for entertaining his many mistresses.

HAMPSHIRE

4 miles (6.4km) north of New Alresford off B3046
OS map 185: ref SU 562362
Open year round (exterior viewing only); entrance free
Wheelchair access, assistance required
Tel: Area office (0892) 48166

GRIMES GRAVES

A strangely eerie feeling pervades the desolate stretch of heathland on the edge of Thetford Forest known as Grimes Graves. This is not an ancient burial ground, as the name might suggest, but an extensive group of flint mines, dating back to the Neolithic period or New Stone Age. The mines were chiefly worked between 2100BC and 1800BC, though some small-scale, open-cast mining continued until about 1650BC.

The site, which has been likened to a war-time bombing range, is dotted with grass-covered hollows, 366 of which can be seen on the surface. Excavations have shown that beneath these hollows are shafts, now completely infilled, cut through sand, boulder clay and chalk. From the bottom of the shaft radiated a number of galleries in which the miners, using antler picks, extracted the high-quality flint or 'floorstone' (a valuable material for tools and weapons) found in bands of chalk. One of the mines is open to the public and, although for safety reasons visitors are not allowed to crawl along the tunnels, it is possible to climb right down the shaft and see its seven galleries. An excellent display area in the custodian's hut describes the history of Grimes Graves and shows how and why the mines were dug, and the custodian is usually on hand to give a fascinating demonstration of the ancient art of flint 'knapping'. When the flint was brought to the surface, knives and other tools were made by 'knapping' — the clever and calculated use of a flint hammerstone to knock off flakes from a large lump of flint.

NORFOLK
7 miles (11.2km) northwest of Thetford off A134
OS map 144: ref TL 818898
Open year round, entrance fee payable
Wheelchair access to exhibition area and grounds only (on rough track)
Tel: Site office (0842) 810656

HELMSLEY CASTLE

Beautifully sited above the town, Helmsley Castle offers excellent views of both the surrounding countryside and the red-tiled roofs of this centuries-old settlement. Its position on an outcrop of rock in the valley of the river Rye must have been a substantial influence on the plan of the castle. The huge earthworks and surviving buildings date (with additions and adaptations) from the Norman Conquest. Its military history was relatively uneventful until it was ruined during the Civil War after a three-month siege in 1644. Today, carefully lawned, the ruins provide a calm and tranquil spot, while those parts of the castle which survive give some idea of the former glory of this once elegant fortress. The keep is quite small and its D-shaped, rather than rectangular, plan is unusual; it has an apse on the east side. Best preserved is the west range, but most interesting are the defences. The north gateway (which once had a portcullis and drawbridge) is flanked by half-round turrets. The castle is surrounded by two ditches and a barbican is mounted on the rampart – good examples of early medieval military planning.

NORTH YORKSHIRE

Near Helmsley town centre on A170
OS map 100: ref SE 611836
Open year round; entrance fee payable
Tel: Site office (0439) 70442

HURST CASTLE

A long shingle spit — a walk of 1½ miles (2.4km) — is the only approach to Hurst Castle other than the local ferry, which operates in summer. Hurst is, in fact, the point on the mainland nearest to the Isle of Wight, but the currents in the Solent are so strong, it is impossible to swim, or even row, across to the castle's site. Curiously, all Hurst's water supply has to be brought over this important stretch of sea, since the castle has no fresh water of its own.

The word 'castle' somewhat understates Hurst's status; it is better described as a fortress. At its heart is the Tudor building, constructed in 1541-4, ordered by Henry VIII as part of his coastal defences. However, Hurst's menacing position is of such strategic military importance that the castle was extensively modernized at the time of the Napoleonic Wars, and again in the mid-nineteenth century when two massive casement wings were added. Even in this century, Hurst has had a role to play: it was garrisoned during both wars. Manned in 1941 by the 129 Coastal Battery Royal Artillery, it remained an important link in Britain's coastal defences until the abolition of the Coastal Artillery branch of the army in 1956. Today, Hurst undoubtedly exudes the atmosphere of a fortress which has been operational for four centuries, and there is plenty of interest to be seen.

Visitors to the castle often make the long trek to the end of the shingle spit to see the rare sea plants which thrive there, and the abundant bird life — terns, oyster-catchers, dippers and even the little-

seen rock pippit. Wildlife also inhabits the castle itself; a kestrel lives inside the walls and starlings nest in the drawbridge chain.

HAMPSHIRE
On Pebble Spit south of Keyhaven OS map 196: ref SZ 319898 Open during summer months, winter weekends only; entrance fee payable Tel: Site office (05904) 2344

JEWEL TOWER, WESTMINSTER

Westminster Abbey and the Houses of Parliament are two of the most popular tourist attractions in London. Every year thousands of eager tourists flock to see these world famous landmarks, little knowing that just a stone's throw away stands one of the least altered medieval buildings in the capital and one of only two complete surviving buildings (the other is Westminster Hall) of the medieval Palace of Westminter. Though moated and constructed of white Kentish rag, the Jewel Tower is easily missed. Its square exterior is overshadowed by the flying buttresses of its magnificent neighbour, Westminster Abbey; yet the interior has its own fascination.

The ground floor, with its unrestored fourteenth-century rib vaulting and grotesque bosses, contains plans of the palace and a reconstruction drawing which shows the position of the Jewel Tower. It also contains an oak wall-plate with elm piles which one supported the building's face. A newel staircase leads to the middle floor, which houses a handsome sword dating from AD800. The door, which dates from 1621, is a reminder of the time when the Tower, no longer used to protect the crown jewels and plate, served as a record office for the House of Lords. From the top there is a unique view of the Victoria Tower, which leads into the House of Lords. On display is a selection of objects found in the moat, including Chinese porcelain, tooth brushes and a pin polisher. There is also an exhibition of weights and measures (including a bushel from Henry VII's time and another from the reign of Elizabeth I), which illustrate the last phase of the tower's working life (1869-1938) when it housed the Board of Trade's Standards Department.

LONDON

St Margaret Street, SW1, opposite south end of Houses of Parliament
Open year round, weekdays; entrance free
Wheelchair access to exterior and ground floor only
Tel: Site office (01) 222 2219

JEWRY WALL

The Jewry Wall is all that survives above ground of the Roman town of Ratae Coritanorum. Despite its rather incongruous situation beside the busy St Nicholas Street, the wall is of great historical importance. Standing 30ft (9m) high, it is one of the largest and best preserved lengths of Roman wall in the country. The origin of its name is not known, but the wall is believed to have been built in AD145-150; it separated the exercise hall of the civic baths from the baths themselves. On the east side of the wall are four arches which would have led through to the baths. Although the site has been greatly disrupted over the years, excavations have helped to uncover the layout of cold bathing area, hot baths, changing rooms, latrine, drainage and heating systems.

A museum adjacent to the site has exhibits of Roman objects found during excavations and informative displays on the wall and civic baths.

LEICESTERSHIRE

In St Nicholas Street, Leicester, west of Church of St Nicholas
OS map 140: ref SK 583044
Open year round; entrance free
Tel: Area office (0902) 765105

Jewry Wall Museum*
St Nicholas Circle, Leicester
Open year round, entrance fee payable
Tel: (0533) 554100

KIRKHAM PRIORY

Most people who pay a visit to one of England's most spectacular residences, Castle Howard, are unaware of the existence of nearby Kirkham Priory. Today only picturesque ruins survive of the once extensive priory, which was built during the mid-eleventh century and gradually enlarged over the next four centuries. The site was once occupied by chambers, halls and a cloister, but the most impressive feature of the surviving masonry is the gatehouse. Built in the late thirteenth century it has a wide gatehall and a range of buildings to the east and the west. The decorative moulding over the door is flanked by statues of St George and the Dragon (east side) and of David and Goliath (west side). Above the door is a figure of Christ within a pointed oval; below stand St Philip and St Bartholomew, in trefoiled niches. Little other than the gateway can be seen, though a small effort of imagination may identify the ground plan of the church, built in the early thirteenth century over the site of an earlier cruciform church.

Kirkham was founded in the twelfth century as a house of Augustinian canons. Interestingly, a significant number of the founder canons decided to join the Cistercian order. Early documentation records an agreement whereby Kirkham Priory was to become a Cistercian house and the canons who wished to remain in the Augustinian order were to move to a new house to be built at Linton. The canons were to take with them all moveable items from Kirkham — crosses, books, chalices, vestments, and even its stained glass. The agreement was never carried out, because the prior who had made it left the house, and Kirkham remained Augustinian until its closure in 1539.

NORTH YORKSHIRE

5 miles (8km) southwest of Malton on minor road off A64
OS map 100: ref SE 735657
Open year round; entrance fee payable
Wheelchair access
Tel: Site office (065381) 768

LANERCOST PRIORY

The impressive west front of the priory church seems rather out of place today in such a quiet, secluded valley, but Lanercost Priory, founded in 1166 as a house for Augustinian canons, was well-endowed and building work was on a grand scale. Most of the red sandstone monastic buildings now stand as handsome ruins, but the nave of the church, which is still intact and used for services, is quite splendid. The west front is a fine example of Early English style and the well-restored interior is quite breathtaking, with three windows in the north aisle which are the work of William Morris and Edward Burne-Jones. Above the west front stands a figure of St Mary Magdalene, the patron saint of the priory. This was carved c. 1270 and is believed to have been a gift from Edward I, who stayed here for six months in 1306-7. The King stopped at Lanercost on his way to Carlisle; illness and bad weather forced his party of 200 to take more permanent shelter. Edward and his queen stayed in the thirteenth-century guest house, part of which can still be seen near the church.

The monastery buildings suffered severely from Scottish raids during the thirteenth and early fourteenth centuries and in 1346 King David II's force ransacked the priory and desecrated the church. The canons attempted to rebuild it, but they incurred heavy debts at every stage. At the dissolution, Lanercost surrendered to Henry VIII in 1542, the property passing on to Sir Thomas Dacre, whose family lived here until 1716. Sir Thomas's tomb is in the north aisle of the church; for reasons not known, the inscription was never completed with the year of his death, 1525.

CUMBRIA

Off minor road south of Lanercost, 2 miles (3.2km) northeast of Brampton
OS map 86: ref NY 556637
Open during summer months; entrance fee payable
Wheelchair access
Tel: Site office (06977) 3030

LAUNCESTON CASTLE

During the early years of the Norman Conquest, Launceston was an important stronghold which controlled the whole area between Bodmin Moor and Dartmoor: today, the castle surveys the grey slate roofs of the pretty town which huddles around it. Its solid motte is topped by an equally solid shell keep and tower, which were designed to be the citadel of the defences. Peering up at the impressive bulk of the tower may induce giddiness, and with good reason — it is leaning to a noticeable degree, and the slant from the horizontal of 3ft 2in (1m) is marked between studs.

The bustling market town of Launceston is well worth browsing around. Its history is interesting (it was, for instance, the site of a mint during Saxon times and was the only walled town in Cornwall) and there are many buildings of note to look out for. Worth particular attention are St Mary Magdelene Church, built in 1542; Church Stile, a fine Georgian house with plastered stucco finish; Blind Hole, a narrow lane whose buildings are constructed on top of the twelfth-century town wall; and Southgate Arch, which is Early English with later additions. Starting with the castle, Launceston offers a fascinating trail of exploration.

CORNWALL

In Launceston, north of A30
OS map 201: ref SX 330846
Open year round, part week only during winter months; entrance fee payable
Wheelchair access to outer bailey
Tel: Site office (0566) 2365

LILLESHALL ABBEY

When you visit Lilleshall Abbey, consider what is beneath your feet. Coal mining in recent times caused considerable subsidence of the whole area, and the ruins of the abbey were put in 'splints' to conserve them. Ruination of the abbey took place during the Civil War, after Sir Richard Leveson made Lilleshall a stronghold against the Roundheads in 1645. Until that time, Lilleshall's history was relatively peaceful. Its original purpose had been to house a community of Arronaisian canons living an austere and contemplative life, and this was the case for four hundred years, until the dissolution of the monasteries under Henry VIII. Income to the abbey was augmented by providing accommodation for travellers passing along the Roman road to the north, Watling Street; Henry III and Richard II had been the abbey's most notable guests.

The remains of the twelfth-century church of the abbey are an impressive sight: the south transept survives, and parts of the east and south ranges. The east processional doorway leading into the cloister buildings is particularly fine. Near this door is an attractive detail — a Romanesque book locker with saw-tooth chevron decoration.

SHROPSHIRE

On unclassified road off A518, 4 miles (6.4km) north of Telford
OS map 127: ref SJ 738142
Open during summer months; entrance fee payable
Wheelchair access
Tel: Site office (0952) 604431

LONGTHORPE TOWER

The exterior of this tower, which adjoins a fourteenth-century manor house, may be somewhat unimpressive, but the treasures inside are quite remarkable. The tower contains a series of fourteenth-century wall paintings, the most complete and the earliest of its kind in England. The paintings, which for centuries had lain hidden but well preserved beneath layers of limewash and distemper, were only discovered in 1945 by the tenant, Mr Hugh Horrell, while redecorating.

The contents of the paintings, with Biblical and domestic scenes, have been taken to represent the contrast between the life of this world and the life of the spirit. One of the most striking paintings is that of philosopher and pupil on the west wall, immediately facing as you enter. Above it is St Anthony and the basket-maker and on the outside arch of the wall there are beautifully detailed birds and scroll-work, and the scant remains of a series showing the labours of the months — digging the soil in March, for example, and killing a pig in December. Other notable paintings are the Nativity scene and the Seven Ages of Man on the north wall and, over the fireplace on the east wall, the Wheel of Five Senses, with a monkey, a vulture, a spider's web, a boar and a cock symbolizing taste, smell, touch, hearing and sight. The paintings are now largely in reds and yellows, although there is evidence that a range of colours was originally used to create a rich and lavish mural decoration. A narrow staircase leads up to the roof of the tower, which overlooks the original, but much restored, manor house (now a private residence) and which offers views of the Nene Valley and Peterborough Cathedral.

CAMBRIDGESHIRE

2 miles (3.2km) west of Peterborough off A47
OS map 142: ref TL 163983
Open year round, part week only; entrance fee payable
Tel: Site office (0733) 268482

LULLINGSTONE ROMAN VILLA

The remains of Lullingstone Villa, which date from the first to the third century, are some of the most impressive in Britain. The intricate mosaics in the Reception Room show Bellerophon killing the Chimaera, decorated with dolphins and patterning of hearts and swastikas and, in the corners, portraits representing the seasons, of which Spring, Summer and Autumn remain. More of the Romans' decorative taste can be seen in the Deep Room, which was devoted to the cult of the local water goddesses. It contains a niche 3ft (90cm) high and 2ft 6in (75cm) wide inside which is a lovely fresco painting of two water nymphs. Originally there were three — a central figure, which survives, flanked by two slightly smaller companions. The painting is well preserved and finely crafted in its detail — green leaves decorate the nymphs' hair, they wear pretty blue necklaces,

and water cascades in stylized patterns from an upturned flagon.

A large number of objects have been found in and around the villa, including a number of marble busts. Larger than lifesize, they are thought to be family likenesses and suggest that a high standard of classical culture was attained even in rural Roman residences. Coins, pots and a number of bronze, glass and bone items have also been discovered — including brooches, pins, dice, glass phials and a bronze axle cap with lion decoration — and some can be seen on display.

KENT
½ mile (0.8km) southeast of Eynsford off A225
OS map 177: ref TQ 529651
Open year round; entrance fee payable
Tel: Site office (0322) 863467

LYDDINGTON BEDE HOUSE

The small, neat village of Lyddington was once a stopping place for the Bishops of Lincoln on their travels around the diocese. Records show that a grand medieval palace stood here as early as the reign of King John (1199-1216) and the bede house building, which dates back to the fifteenth century, was originally part of that palace; two rooms on the first floor were clearly the bishop's audience chamber and private chamber. After the Reformation, the property passed to Thomas, Lord of Burghley, who converted it into an almshouse in 1602, hence the name bede house: 'bede' comes from the word 'biddan', to pray, as everyone who was given charity was expected to pray in thanks to their benefactors. (A later meaning has it as the equivalent of 'bead', also representing a prayer.) The original 'ordynaunces' for the foundation, dated March 1601, are on display in the entrance hall and make fascinating reading.

Built of honey-coloured local limestone dressed with darker stone, the bede house has large mullioned windows and a steep roof covered with Collyweston slates. It continued as an almshouse until earlier this century and today the rooms, although unfurnished, are extremely well preserved. The main attraction is the great hall, with its elaborate and beautifully carved early sixteenth-century timber ceiling, oriel window and open fireplace. Leading off the great hall is the bishop's privy chamber, fitted with the most modern conveniences for the time: a latrine and washing closet with a stone sink and metal basin, complete with soap dish.

The bede house stands to the west of Lyddington Church, a handsome and spacious fifteenth-century building. The position of the altar, some distance from the east wall and surrounded by rails, is the legacy of an early seventeenth-century ecclesiastical dispute between Anglicans and Puritans.

LEICESTERSHIRE

In Lyddington 6 miles (9.6km) north of Corby
OS map 141: ref SP 875970
Open during summer months; entrance fee payable
Wheelchair access to ground-floor rooms only
Tel: Site office (057282) 2438

MARBLE HILL HOUSE

A pleasant riverside walk leads from Richmond Bridge, with its views of Richmond Hill, where many artists have set up their easels to paint the terrace gardens and the valley of the Thames, to the splendid Palladian villa known as Marble Hill House. The house was built for George II's mistress, Henrietta Howard, later Countess of Suffolk, who was said by Lord Hervey (as recorded by Horace Walpole) to have 'good sense, good breeding and good nature . . . which even her enemies could not deny her'.

Built in 1724-9, Marble Hill House is attributed to Lord Herbert, an amateur architect acquainted with the works of Andrea Palladio (1508-80). The house may have had a complicated 'birth', with many hands wishing to make their mark: it seems that the builder, Roger Morris, was engaged to construct only 'the naked carcass of a house'. But whatever the complications of construction, and indeed of finance (work stopped for some three years when Henrietta was unable to keep up payments), the result is a perhaps surprisingly modest interior encased in an undeniably fine exterior. In all, Marble Hill is a lovely house in a beautiful setting.

LONDON

On Richmond Road, A305 between Twickenham and Richmond
Open year round; entrance free
Wheelchair access
Tel: Site office (01) 892 5115

MIDDLEHAM CASTLE

The massive bulk of Middleham Castle leaves no doubt that it was built as a major defence for rich and important people and it is, indeed, the third-largest surviving English keep. The first castle on the site was a motte-and-bailey fortress and its earthworks, which can still be seen, are known locally as 'William's Hill'. In 1170 Robert Fitzralf began work constructing this impressive stronghold on the site. The castle began to come to real prominence as the property of the Neville family, including Richard, Earl of Warwick, known as Warwick the Kingmaker. It was here that the young man later to become Richard III of England was sent to learn the knightly arts — it was to be his only settled home. When he was just eighteen, Richard was given Middleham by his brother, Edward IV, for loyal service. Richard married Lady Anne, Warwick's youngest daughter, and their only son Edward was born and died here.

It was during Richard's tenure that Middleham came into its prime, as the 'Lord of the North' ruled on behalf of his brother. Richard took the throne in 1483, but he was to reign for only two years. When he died at the Battle of Bosworth in 1485, the ruling line of Plantagenets came to an end and Henry Tudor became King Henry VII. Thereafter the castle gradually declined and though parish records show that it was still occupied during the seventeenth century, it eventually fell into disrepair and its stone was looted by local people. (It is easy to spot stone from Middleham, especially its fine ashlar-stone facing, on seventeenth and eighteenth century buildings in the neighbourhood). Nevertheless, there is still plenty to see of this fine fortress: the keep, whose walls are near their original height, the banqueting hall, the thirteenth-century chapel, the fourteenth-century gatehouse and the deep moat.

NORTH YORKSHIRE

At Middleham, 2 miles (3.2km) south of Leyburn on A6108
OS map 99: ref SE 128875
Open year round; entrance fee payable
Tel: Site office (0969) 23899

MINSTER LOVELL HALL

Surprisingly, the picturesque ruins of Minster Lovell Hall were brought into being by one of its later owners, Thomas Coke, who on building a new mansion at Holkham in Norfolk, simply abandoned his former residence. On his orders, Minster Lovell Hall was dismantled, with just a few rooms being converted into farm buildings.

Today the hall, its dovecote and the nearby small parish church provide an attractive huddle of buildings on the bank of the river Windrush. The manor was arranged around a quadrangle open to the river on the south side. The principle remains are the great hall, with its entrance porch, and the southwest tower situated beside the river. The church, built by William Cowell (whose effigy can be seen inside) was founded in the ninth century and is much better preserved. From the church — the 'minster' — both the hall and the village take their names; Lovell was added in the thirteenth century to distinguish the Lovell family's manor from that of the Earl of Pembroke,

the adjacent manor of Little Minster. The manorial dovecote dates from medieval times, when it provided an important source of fresh meat during the winter months. Stooping low, you can enter this small circular building and, when accustomed to the darkness, take a look at its walls lined with nesting boxes and its conical roof.

Pleasant walks from Minster Lovell abound. A public footpath leads across the fields to Crawley, and on to the market town of Witney. Another walk passes behind the church, through the meadows and along the river down the beautiful Windrush Valley. A winter visit to Minster Lovell is a particular delight, when snow and frost turn the surroundings into a fairytale spectacle.

OXFORDSHIRE

3 miles (4.8km) west of Witney on minor road off B4047
OS map 164: ref SP 324114
Open year round; entrance free
Tel: Site office (0993) 75315

MISTLEY TOWERS

Sawmills, timber yards, maltings and corn wharves all thrived in Mistley during the nineteenth century and the village remains an active, if small, port. It has an ancient heritage dating back to Norman times, when it was known as Mitleslea. The name came from 'mircel' (the herb now known as basil) and 'ley' (pasture). The area was owned during the eighteenth century by the Rigby family. Richard Rigby, a notoriously corrupt politician, had the grand notion to turn the place into a spa. Perhaps fortunately his plans failed to come to fruition; but he was responsible for the building of Mistley Towers. They are the work of Robert Adam, all that remains of the church he designed for Mistley and one of only two surviving examples of his ecclesiastical architecture.

When the church was demolished, the twin towers were saved for use as mausolea. Inside one of them there is a memorial to Richard Rigby and a list of the Ten Commandments including, of course, 'Thou shalt not steal'. Interesting to note, then, that at Rigby's death in 1788 he was found to have amassed about half-a-million pounds out of his public services: but in the eighteenth century, it must be said, such accruals were not strictly regarded as 'stealing'.

ESSEX
On B1352, 1½ miles (2.4km) east of A137 at Lawford, 9 miles (14.4km) east of Colchester
OS map 169: ref TM 116320
Open year round; key obtained on site
Wheelchair access to exterior only
Tel: Area office (0223) 358911

MOUNT GRACE PRIORY

Mount Grace's full title is impressive — the House of the Assumption of the Most Blessed Virgin and St Nicholas of Mount Grace at Ingleby. It was founded by Thomas de Holand and licensed by the Crown in 1398. A stipulation of its foundation charter was that the monks should pray for the royal family; but as Richard II was deposed before building work was even begun, ownership of the priory was in constant dispute for more than a century. Its fate was ultimately the same as that of many other priories and abbeys: Mount Grace fell victim to the dissolution in December 1539.

Today, trees completely screen the picturesque priory ruins from the nearby motorway, so that its secluded setting retains something of the atmosphere in which its hermit-like occupants once lived. Members of the Carthusian order, the monks lived isolated not only from the outside world, but also from one another. Each monk lived in his own cell, receiving food through a service hatch which had a right-angled bend to prevent the server and the cell inmate from seeing one another; examples of these hatches can be seen along the east and south walls of the great cloister. Along the south side of the cloister are the remains of the prior's cell in which the fine moulded corbelling of what was once an oriel window survives; of the frater (or dining room) which was used on Sundays and during festivals, the doorway of which has shields bearing the arms of Redman quartering Aldburgh; and of the chapterhouse, which leads into the church (the foundations of the high altar are visible beside the east wall). Walking through the ruins evokes strong feelings of the space and organization of the Carthusian order. Indeed, the extensive remains at Mount Grace offer the best opportunity in England to study the Carthusian plan.

NORTH YORKSHIRE

7 miles (11.2km) northeast of Northallerton on A19
OS map 99: ref SE 453982
Open year round; entrance fee payable
Wheelchair access
Tel: Site office (0609) 23249

MUCHELNEY ABBEY

Winding, narrow Somerset lanes lead exploring visitors to Muchelney Abbey. A notice at the entrance invites them to ring the hand-bell, and the attendant who answers its echoing peel shows them into the abbot's lodgings. The lodgings survived the dissolution intact because they offered a convenient home for the new owner of the abbey, Edward Seymour, brother-in-law to Henry VIII. The coffered oak ceilings, finely carved doors, stone fireplaces, linenfold panelling, wooden benching, decorative arcading and fan vaulting — all well preserved — show why it would have been an attractive prospect as a private residence. Just visible, too, are the faded chevron and ermine motifs of a painted fresco. Outside, the ruins are well displayed amid carefully maintained lawns and it is relatively easy to distinguish the main shapes of the cloister and church, including the Lady Chapel, nave and radiating chapels (off the ambulatory).

As for the abbey's pre-dissolution history, the Charter of Kynewulf in AD762 mentions an abbey and names one Edwold as its abbot. But it is thought that the abbey is even older, and was perhaps founded by King Ine c.697. At that time the area was extremely marshy, with just one or two places above flood level; indeed, the name 'Muchelney' means 'the Great Island' (even today the abbey is sometimes inaccessible in winter). The abbey was refounded in AD939 by King Aethelstan, after the Viking invasions but the buildings preserved here are thought to date from a later period, after the Norman Conquest.

SOMERSET

At Muchelney 2 miles (3.2km) south of Langport
OS map 193: ref ST 428248
Open year round, part week only; entrance fee payable
Wheelchair access to part of ground floor only
Tel: Site office (0458) 250664

NETLEY ABBEY

Eighteenth-century engravings by Samuel and Nathaniel Buck show Netley to have been even then a ruin, covered in weeds and wild flowers, and it was described by a devotee of the Romantic movement as 'inspiring the most pleasing melancholy'. Today, little has changed, although the pleasure is perhaps more evident than the melancholy. The encroaching flora have been removed and daisy-dotted lawns have replaced tangled shrubs and trailing ivy, but the abbey is essentially still a place of romantic atmosphere.

Officially called the Abbey of St Mary of Edwardstow, which implies a dedication to Edward the Confessor, the original name of the abbey was Letley (Letelie in the Domesday survey, Lettelage in the Charter of 1251), which became corrupted into Netley. It owed its existence to Peter des Roches, Bishop of Winchester from 1204 to 1238, and to Henry III, who assumed the duties of founder patron in March 1251. The king's name

is on the base of the northeast great pier of the crossing in the abbey church (and is now protected by a small transparent plaque).

After dissolution in 1536, the buildings and site were granted to Sir William Paulet (later Marquis of Winchester) who converted the church into a substantial house, thus saving much of the fabric of the abbey which can be seen today. Visitors can wander among the ruined remains of the church, cloister, east range (library and sacristy), chapterhouse, monks' parlour, sub-vault of the dorter, reredorter and south range.

HAMPSHIRE

In Netley, 7 miles (11.2km) southeast of Southampton, facing Southampton Water
OS map 196: ref SU 453089
Open during summer months, weekends only in winter; entrance fee payable
Wheelchair access
Tel: Site office (0703) 453076

NORHAM CASTLE

The ruins of Norham Castle were a favourite subject for the painter J.M.W. Turner. Throughout his lifetime he made many studies of this massive castle, which stands majestically above the river Tweed, its walls of local pink stone creating a mellow glow in the sunlight. Behind the beauty of the castle and the setting, however, lies a turbulent past — during the fourteenth century Norham Castle was described as the 'most dangerous and adventurous place in the country'.

The castle was originally built *c*. 1121 by the royal chancellor, Bishop Ranulph Flambard. It was then rebuilt some fifty years later by Bishop Hugh of Puiset. It became a major border stronghold and for the next four centuries was gradually reconstructed and strengthened to keep up with advances in military tactics. It survived so many sieges and attacks that at one time it was thought to be impregnable, but in 1513 the castle was successfully stormed and partially destroyed by James IV on his way to the Battle of Flodden. Although extensively altered, it had lost its importance by the end of the sixteenth century and gradually became more and more ruinous.

The most substantial remains date back to the fifteenth and sixteenth centuries, but half of the twelfth-century keep is still standing. Simple and restrained in design, it is one of the most impressive of its period. The main entrance is through the gate tower to the west, which is known as 'Marmions's Gate' after an English knight, Sir William Marmion, who single-handedly took on the Scots during a prolonged siege in 1319. Marmion had been given a helmet with a golden crest by his lady-love with instruction to take it to 'the most dangerous place in Britain and there make it famous'. He headed for Norham and, when, four days after his arrival, a strong party of Scottish horsemen came to the castle, Marmion mounted his horse, galloped through the west gate and charged them. Luckily he was saved by back-up forces who chased the enemy across the river. Sir William became the hero of Sir Walter Scott's epic poem, *Marmion*:

> *Day set on Norham's castled steep,*
> *And Tweed's fair river, broad and deep,*
> *And Cheviot's mountains lone:*
> *The battled towers, the donjon keep,*
> *The loophole grates where captives weep,*
> *The flanking walls that round it sweep,*
> *In yellow lustre shone.*

NORTHUMBERLAND

Norham village, 6½ miles (10.4km) southwest of Berwick-upon-Tweed on minor road off B6470 (from A698)
OS map 75: ref NT 907476
Open year round part week only during winter months
Wheelchair access except to castle keep
Tel: Site office (028982) 329

NORTH LEIGH ROMAN VILLA

Crowds of tourists flock daily to Blenheim Palace, the famous birthplace of Sir Winston Churchill; few find their way to North Leigh ancient monument, just 4 miles (6.4km) away. North Leigh, it is true, is not easily accessible, and there is a half-mile (0.8km) walk down an unpaved road from the site's parking area.

North Leigh is one of a group of Romano-British farms and country houses in the lower valleys of the Glyme and Evenlode which have been revealed by aerial photography. Excavation has disclosed a substantial number of individual rooms, and the 'footprint' remains of the living quarters and baths arranged around a courtyard can be seen today. It is evident that North Leigh villa was prosperous and that produce from its fertile land found a ready market in the major Roman towns to which it was connected by road.

The most attractive of the remains is undoubtedly the mosaic flooring of the great dining room, which dates from the fourth century. So many mosaics have been removed to museums for safe keeping; this fine example can be viewed in its original situation. Its pattern is composed of four colours: red (tile), blue (liassic limestone containing iron), grey and white (both types of limestone). The floor was heated by a hypocaust system and flues were connected to the underfloor space to provide vents for smoky air to escape. The brick pillars of this system can be seen through a hole in the south corner of the room.

Interesting footpaths across the land once harvested by the Romans lead to Comb and Stonesfield.

OXFORDSHIRE
9 miles (14.4km) west of Oxford off A4095 OS map 164: ref SP 397154 Open year round, part week only; entrance fee payable Tel: Site office (0993) 881830

NUNNEY CASTLE

In the midst of the grey stone buildings of the charming Somerset village of Nunney, beside the bubbling village stream, stands the tall and impressive shell of Nunney Castle. Strategically, its position in a valley must have been far from ideal, but for visitors it is a delight.

Nunney Castle, essentially a tower house, was built in 1373 by Sir John de la Mare after his return, much the richer, from the wars in France. It is a single block, rectangular in shape with circular towers at each corner, and has a strong French influence to its design, most notably demonstrated in the machicolations by which the wall walk was corbelled out beyond the line of the walls. Nunney Castle stands within a very constricted moat area; in fact, the moat originally came right up to the castle walls and was crossed by a fixed bridge, which stood at the site of the present bridge.

Nunney Castle was besieged in the Civil War and the garrison's brave efforts (apparently they tortured their last surviving pig every day to make it sound as it were being slaughtered, to convince the enemy there was plenty to eat) were to no avail. The north side was weakened by cannon fire and later 'slighted' under Cromwell's orders, rendering it useless. The walls were left standing, but the floors and partitions were removed. The castle was never reoccupied and although the north wall has now collapsed, three sides and the towers stand at their full height.

SOMERSET

In Nunney, 3½ miles (5.6km) southwest of Frome, off A361
OS map 183: ref ST 737457
Open year round; entrance free
Wheelchair access to exterior only
Tel: Area office (0272) 734472

ODDA'S CHAPEL

Earl Odda ordered this royal chapel to be built and dedicated in honour of the Holy Trinity for the good of the soul of his brother Elfric who died in this place. Bishop Ealdred dedicated it on April 12th in the 14th year of the reign of Edward, King of the English

Thus reads the text of the original dedication stone inside this attractive pre-Conquest chapel built for Earl Odda, a kinsman and personal friend of Edward the Confessor. The inscription fixes the date as 1056, and the chapel is unusual in that it is one of only two pre-Conquest chapels in rural England to be found in the same village as a Saxon church (Heysham in Lancashire is the other).

The simple beauty of Odda's Chapel is well described in a verse from *The Little Sanctuary* by Admiral R.A. Hopwood:

And I chanced upon the chapel when the world was full of strife
Entered there, to rest in silence and alone,

And its spirit bore me backwards just as far from modern life
As the name of Odda graven on its stone.

The chapel's plain nave and square-ended chancel are divided by a 10ft (3m) high chancel arch. The chancel itself is now incomplete; part has been sectioned off to form an attractive half-timbered private house, which can be viewed from the chapel grounds. But despite alterations over the centuries — windows have been cut, an upper floor inserted, a fireplace and doorway blocked up, a wall demolished — its original character can still be sensed, and it remains a peaceful refuge.

GLOUCESTERSHIRE

In Deerhurst, off B4213, at Abbot's Court, southwest of parish church
OS map 150: ref SO 869298
Open year round; entrance free
Tel: Area office (0272) 734472

OKEHAMPTON CASTLE

First mentioned in the Domesday Book, Okehampton Castle has a fascinating history of royal occupation, baronial rule and aristocratic life-style. Yet today, despite never having been under siege, it is more like a sculpture garden than a fortress. Its crumbling ruins rise steeply up the hillside, culminating in a keep situated on a high mound whose sides sweep down to the river West Okement. From the surviving fragments of wall, it is possible to identify the barbican tower (early fourteenth century), the great hall (mainly early fourteenth century), the chapel and the postern gate (early fourteenth century) and the keep (late eleventh century and early fourteenth century). Each wall is a fascinating 'pattern book' of fireplaces, openings, joist holes and floor beam sockets.

There is a panoramic view over the historic town of Okehampton and a good supply of well-placed benches. There is also a path known as Lady Howard's Walk, which passes around the castle's boundary, and which is at its best in late May, when great 'lakes' of bluebells swathe the banks and cover the footpath itself. The ghost of Lady Howard is said to travel from Tavistock in a coach made from the bones of her four murdered husbands and drawn by headless horses, accompanied by a dog who eats one blade of grass at midnight! In early summer the mound on which the castle stands is covered with bluebells and local people traditionally visit Okehampton Castle on the first Sunday in June to admire their display and the other wild flowers.

DEVON

1 mile (1.6km) southwest of Okehampton off A30
OS map 191: ref SX 584942
Open year round, part week only during winter; entrance fee payable
Tel: Area office (0272) 734472

OLD MERCHANT'S HOUSE AND ROW 111 HOUSES: GREAT YARMOUTH

Hidden in narrow streets, called 'rows', and often overlooked by sun-seeking visitors to Great Yarmouth, are two beautifully restored houses, the Old Merchant's House and the now combined houses, numbers 7 and 8, Row 111. Together these buildings act as a showcase for displays of local architectural and domestic fittings and tell the fascinating story of the rise and fall of the row area of Great Yarmouth from the seventeenth century to the twentieth.

A medieval walled town, Great Yarmouth became prosperous after the mid-sixteenth century, when great shoals of herring changed their pattern of migration and began to appear on the east coast of England. The impact of this new-found wealth on the population, and the destruction caused by a fire in 1571, led to a complete rebuilding of the town. The medieval town plan was retained, with a series of narrow alleys, or 'rows', leading off three main streets. The row houses, which varied in size according to the wealth and status of the owner, were of a very specialized type: walls of brick and flint, tiled roofs, and large wooden windows with leaded lights.

The row area was a pleasantly light and well-sheltered place to live; some of the houses had small gardens. However, the building of many new houses in the eighteenth and nineteenth centuries turned the area into a slum. The rows were largely demolished by bomb damage during World War II, and later redeveloped; but these two houses have been preserved and furnished with fittings salvaged from other row houses.

The Old Merchant's House is an example of the larger dwellings of the wealthy merchants. Built c. 1604, it is spaciously grand and has been refitted with beautiful windows. The ceilings are high and often decorated with elaborate plasterwork. On display is a fine collection of ornamental wall anchors.

Numbers 7 and 8, Row 111 were originally one house, built in the early seventeenth century, with two rooms on each of the three floors. It was later divided into three separate, tiny dwellings for the less well-to-do fisher-folk. Throughout are collections of local fitments, including doors, pannelling, fireplaces, cupboards, latches and knockers. Entrance to these houses is by guided tour only, lasting around half an hour and leaving at regular intervals from Numbers 7 and 8, Row 111. The tour ends with a visit to another English Heritage property, Greyfriars' Cloisters, the remains of a thirteenth-century Franciscan friary

with fragments of a fourteenth-century wall painting in the crypt.

NORFOLK
In Great Yarmouth, off South Quay
OS map 134: Houses ref TG 525072; Cloisters ref TG 525073
Open year round, admission on guided tour only; entrance fee payable
Tel: Site office (0493) 857900

OLD SARUM

Spectacular views of Salisbury and its famous cathedral make the windy walk around Old Sarum a delight. Standing 400ft (122m) above sea level and about 240ft (73m) above the river Avon, Old Sarum has been the site of hill forts, castles, cathedrals and a palace. Hand-axes of the Old Stone Age have been found, and the first evidence of permanent settlement is from the early Iron Age. The site is enclosed by the massive earthworks of an Iron Age fort, and it was continuously occupied, successively, by the Romans, Saxons and Normans. The peak of activity was after the Norman Conquest, when building of a royal castle at the centre and a cathedral to the northwest was begun. The cathedral was completed in 1092 by St Osmund, but just five days after its consecration it was destroyed by a storm. Only the nave survived, and this was incorporated into the next cathedral, built by Bishop Roger. Outlines of both cathedrals can be seen today. Apart from the crumbling remains of Bishop Roger's palace, there is little to see except the grassy mound itself; but this is spectacular, and there is an indefinable and undeniably special atmosphere about Old Sarum.

WILTSHIRE
2 miles (3.2km) north of Salisbury
OS map 184: ref SU 138327
Open year round; entrance fee payable
Wheelchair access to inner bailey and grounds only
Tel: Area office (0272) 734472

ORFORD CASTLE

Work began on Orford Castle in 1165 and was
completed in 1173 at a total cost of £1413 9s 2d.
The fact that these exact figures are known is
important; Orford is the earliest castle in Great
Britain with detailed records of building and costs.
It was commissioned by Henry II as a Royal
stronghold and coastal defence, the first and most
powerful in East Anglia, using techniques in
military architecture very advanced for the period.
Square towers placed at intervals along the wall,
for example, were an innovation in defence
tactics. The massive 90ft (27.4m) tall keep, which
towers above the picturesque Suffolk village of
Orford, is just about all that remains above
ground; the last surviving portion of the wall
collapsed in 1841 'with a tremendous crash'.
Unusual in design, it consists of a tall tower with
three rectangular towers spaced at equal distances
around the outside. The external wall is
polygonal, but inside the rooms are circular. It is
still intact, with all three main floors accessible to
visitors. In the upper hall there is an exhibition
covering the history of the castle and coastline.
The staircase leads to the modern flat roof of the
great tower, which offers spectacular and
wonderfully windswept views over Orford and
Orford Ness, the sea and the surrounding
countryside.

During the summer months, Orford Castle is
often the setting for the re-enactment of the local
legend of the Orford merman, an integral part of
the castle's history. The merman, so the story
goes, was caught by local fisherman shortly after
the castle was completed. A wild and naked man,
covered with hair and shaggy beard, he was kept a
prisoner and tortured for not speaking (often hung
by his feet), and when taken to church he showed
no reverence. Eventually his captors took him
back to sea, guarding him closely; but he dived
under the nets and came up the other side to mock
the onlookers. Just as everyone had given up hope
of catching him again, he came back to the nets of
his own free will. The merman was taken back to
the castle, but later fled to sea and was never seen
again.

SUFFOLK

In Orford, off B1084, 20 miles (32km) northeast of Ipswich
OS map 169: ref TM 419499
Open year round, part week only during winter months;
   entrance fee payable
Wheelchair access to exterior only
Tel: Area office (0223) 358911

PICKERING CASTLE

At the time of the Norman Conquest there was a manor on this site which was popular with medieval kings, who were keen to hunt in the extensive woodland which surrounded the area. The manor was visited three times by William I. The castle was probably established during William's reign (1066-1087) and extended during the twelfth and thirteenth centuries. It stands on a limestone bluff and was built from limestone and wood cut from the nearby forest. Pickering is of special interest because the use of timber in its defences continued until the fourteenth century; it was the work of bondmen and socmen (tenants) to keep it in good repair. Pickering was visited by most English sovereigns between 1100 and 1400 (appreciation of the excellent hunting continued). Over the centuries Pickering was, however, poorly maintained, as a mid-sixteenth century itinerary drawn up by the Royal Antiquary, John Leland, reveals:

> Thens to Pykering: the Castelle stondith in an end of the town not far from the paroch church on the brow of the hille, under the which the broke rennith. In the first court it be a 4. toures, of the which one is callid Rosamunde's Toure. In the ynner court be also a 4. toures, whereof the keep is one. The castelle waulles and the toures be meatly welle, the logginges be in ruin . . .

Today the ruins of Pickering provide the visitor with an unusually good indication of the castle's original size and layout, including the bailey ditch of the Norman castle; the Coleman Tower — known during the fourteenth century as 'the king's prison' (it is noted in a fifteenth century verse that Richard II was imprisoned briefly at Pickering before his murder); the splendid motte and shell keep; the hall; the chapel — first mentioned in 1227 when a chalice and two vestments were provided for it; the constable's lodgings; Rosamund's Tower — perhaps named after one of Henry II's mistresses, the 'fair Rosamund', who died more than a century before the tower was built; and Diete Hill Tower — which may take its name from the Middle English word 'diet', meaning 'a day's work', possibly referring to a feudal duty to give a number of days' labour.

A visit to nearby Beck Isle Museum of Rural Life will reveal what the castle looked like earlier this century. In this fascinating and crowded museum you can see photographs taken during the 1920s, when Pickering Castle was partly concealed by a thick growth of trees and bushes.

NORTH YORKSHIRE

In Pickering, 15 miles (24km) southwest of Scarborough
OS map 100: ref SE 800845
Open year round; entrance fee payable
Wheelchair access except to motte
Tel: Site office (0751) 74989

Beck Isle Museum of Rural Life*, Pickering
Open April-October; entrance fee payable
Tel: (0751) 73653

PIEL CASTLE

Piel Island, with its handful of houses and inn (worth a visit for the ducks, peacocks and guinea fowl kept there, and the goat which runs to greet visitors) guards the narrow channel to Barrow harbour. Windswept and continuously battered by a frothing sea, Piel Island can be a daunting place to reach; indeed, except in summer months it may too difficult for the ferry to make the crossing.

Built some 600 years ago by the Abbot of Furness to protect the abbey against raids from the Scots, Piel Castle in fact fulfilled a second purpose. It was an ideal storage place for goods traded with the Irish on the black market. Though it is ruined, the castle offers plenty to explore. Most notable is the keep (which can be clearly seen from the mainland) with its four corner turrets. But there are also the remains of the towers, two courts, and a porch which has grooves for a portcullis.

There is a road-causeway leading to Roa Island which was built originally by a railway company to service trade with Irish cattle boats; the last train ran in 1934.

CUMBRIA

On Piel Island, 3½ miles (5.6km) southeast of Barrow-in-Furness
OS map 96: ref SD 233636
Open year round; entrance free
Access by ferry from Roa Island; regular service weekends, weekdays by arrangement only; inaccessible during poor weather
Tel: Ferry service (0229) 26284

PORTCHESTER CASTLE

Above a spit of land jutting into Portsmouth
Harbour stand the remains of Portchester Castle,
its centrepiece the impressive Norman Keep built
by Henry I. The castle is unusual in that it is set
within the walls of a large Roman fort. Built in the
third century, the fort was one of the 'Saxon
Shore' forts, a chain of defences (described in an
exhibition sited in the castle keep) which
protected the southeast coast of England from
attack by Saxon pirates. The walls of the Roman
fort still stand at their full height of 18ft (5.4m)
and are complete on four sides. The best view of
the extensive fortress is gained from the medieval
Land Gate; from here a path leads across the
grassed outer bailey to the second entrance, the
Water Gate, which can also be approached by
boat at high tide.

The castle remains stand within a moated inner
bailey at the Land Gate end of the outer bailey.
They are dominated by the tall, square keep,
where visitors can climb to the top and enjoy both
the view of the layout of the castle buildings
within the fortress and the sweeping panorama of
Portsmouth Harbour.

The castle was modernized by Richard II at the
end of the fourteenth century. He converted it
into a small palace, a project he was so keen to
finish that work took place by day and night. The
remains of the hall, kitchen and great chamber
still stand. The castle, long popular with royal
visitors and a useful embarkation point — Edward
III gathered his troops here before the Battle of
Crécy, and Henry V did so before the Battle of
Agincourt — was also used as a military prison,
latterly for French seamen during the Napoleonic
Wars. To hold as many as 5000 prisoners, timber
huts were erected in the outer enclosure. Prisoners
inscribed their names in the walls of the keep, and
many of these, with dates from the early
eighteenth century, can still be seen quite clearly.
At the opposite end of the outer bailey there is a
small twelfth-century church once part of an
Augustinian priory, founded in 1133 by William
Pont d'Arch, with the help of Henry I. The monks
stayed there only fifteen years, but their church
has been well preserved and the west front and
twelfth-century carved font are notable features.

HAMPSHIRE
On the south side of Portchester off A27
OS map 196: ref SU 625046
Open year round; entrance fee payable
Wheelchair access to grounds and lower levels only
Tel: Site office (0705) 378291

PORTLAND CASTLE

Portland Castle, one of a string of coastal defences constructed in the reign of Henry VIII, is tightly wedged between Ministry of Defence property and a naval base and provides an opportunity to compare Tudor military organization with today's efforts. The castle was built c. 1540 to defend against the possibility of invasion from France and Spain. It continued to be useful through the centuries: it occupied a strategic position during the Civil War, was seized by royalists in 1642, and changed hands twice in 1643; it was a prison for political prisoners (Lauderdale, a counsellor of Charles II, was held here); a plan of 1725 notes its use to protect trading ships against privateers; and it served as officers' quarters during the late nineteenth century and as an ordnance store for the Royal Naval Air Service.

Visitors today can see the soldiers' barracks, the battery, the great hall, the kitchen and pantry, the cellar and the gun room and store rooms. In the entrance hall there is a sturdy column known as the whipping post, where miscreants were flogged. The castle bell is called the 'Portland Muster', because if the castle came under threat and the bell was tolled, all men from sixteen to sixty had to come to the rescue armed with whatever they could muster. The first time it was rung, in 1542, seventy-six men — fifty armed with bow and arrows and six with pikes — responded. Like many other castles, Portland is said to have its resident spirit, a lady dressed in a green Tudor costume. She has been seen during the day and night, but no one knows her identity.

DORSET
Overlooking Portland Harbour OS map 194: ref SY 684743 Open year round, part week only; entrance fee payable Wheelchair access to exterior and ground floor only Tel: Site office (0305) 820539

PRIOR'S HALL BARN, WIDDINGTON

For those interested in English architecture, Prior's Hall Barn, one of the finest surviving medieval barns in East Anglia, is essential viewing. A large, aisled barn, constructed to provide corn storage, it is typical for the area but it does have some peculiar features which have survived with little alteration since the fourteenth century. Prior's Hall Barn was built with 'green' oak which seasoned in position, resulting in the many twisted timbers which can be seen. The notches in the aisle posts indicate where the largest timbers were propped during construction. A rare survival from the fourteenth century are the cusped bargeboards of the porches which, together with the curved braces in the walls and inside framing, give the overall feel of the Decorated period of English architecture.

The history of the barn is interesting, too. It was built on land given by William the Conqueror to the priory of St Valéry-sur-Somme, which established a daughter house at Warish Hall — hence the name, Prior's Hall Barn (Widdington means 'willow farm'). Nothing remains from this early period, but it is thought that a barn may have occupied the present site. In 1379 the possessions of St Valéry, including this site, were seized by Edward III; Prior's Hall was then acquired by Bishop William of Wykeham, who gave it as an endowment to New College, Oxford, which he founded in the same year. The barn which can be seen today was probably built by New College, who held it for the next five-and-a-half centuries.

ESSEX
In Widdington, on unclassified road 2 miles (3.2km) southeast of Newport OS map 167: ref TL 538319 Open weekends during summer months only; entrance fee payable Wheelchair access Tel: Site office (0799) 41047

PRUDHOE CASTLE

The extensive remains of this twelfth-century castle stand on a powerful site — a wooded spur which drops steeply to the river Tyne (Prudhoe means 'proud hill'). Prudhoe Castle is not particularly large, but with massive walls 26ft (7.9m) high and more than 5ft (1.5m) thick, its exceptional strength made the castle one of the most important in the country during the Middle Ages. It held out successfully against two sieges, in 1173 and 1174, from King William of Scotland, surviving 'without a pennyworth of harm', and did not fall until Oliver Cromwell destroyed the tower with cannon fire.

Prudhoe Castle was originally built as an earth-and-timber defence by the Umfravilles, barons of Prudhoe, c.1100. A stone curtain wall (much of which is still standing) was added in the late twelfth century and it was further strengthened in the following 200 years. The splendid gatehouse is the oldest surviving part of the castle, dating from the early twelfth century, the same period as the now ruined keep. Above the passageway is a stone vault, supported on both sides by corbel stones featuring carvings of a pair of human heads. A steep stairway leads up to a room which was converted into a chapel in the thirteenth century. The oriel window above the altar is thought to be one of the earliest in England. Above the chapel was the guardroom, in which the crossloops which controlled the barbican passage are still visible.

A Georgian manor house dominates the inner courtyard of the castle. Built in the early nineteenth century by the second Duke of Northumberland, it stands on the site of a range of medieval buildings and some of the interior walls date back to that time. It is a handsome, well-proportioned building which now contains an informative exhibition on the history of the castle and manor house. The grounds are beautiful and worth exploring.

NORTHUMBERLAND

In Prudhoe, on minor road off A695
OS map 88: ref NZ 092634
Open year round, part week only during winter months; entrance fee payable
Tel: Site office (0661) 33459

RESTORMEL CASTLE

Approached through a short avenue of rhododendron bushes, Restormel is a picturesque sight, especially in the spring when it is surrounded by banks of daffodils and bluebells. Chiefly, visitors see the remains of the keep, but the importance of Restormel is that it was a petrified motte, and even the surviving construction gives an excellent impression of what this was intended to look like. That the ruins call to mind the structure of the Roman Colosseum is only coincidental with the fact that one of Restormel's earliest owners, Richard, Earl of Cornwall, held the title 'King of the Romans', as the heir designate of the Holy Roman Empire.

From the wall walk of the keep, the layout of the castle can be identified. Within this circular shell there is a series of apartments which surround a courtyard, and also a kitchen with a massive fireplace, the great hall, solar, chapel and a bedchamber. Restormel's interesting history dates from c. 1100. It was visited by Edward the Black Prince and during the Civil War was garrisoned by the Parliamentarian forces of Lord Essex. Today, its high walls give broad views of the surrounding pasture land. The castle is set in attractive grounds and the moat is carpeted with primroses in spring.

CORNWALL
1½ miles (2.4km) north of Lostwithiel off A390
OS map 200: ref SX 104614
Open year round, part week only; entrance fee payable
Tel: Site office (020887) 2687

RICHBOROUGH CASTLE

Now standing in rather bleak, flat landscape, Richborough Castle was originally the Roman fort of Rutupiae. It was here that the Roman invasion army landed in AD43 and established a temporary base, and from here that the Romans built Watling Street, the road that led to London and on to Chester. In Roman times, the fort lay on a small peninsula jutting into the river Wantsum, which separated Thanet from the mainland of Kent. As the area became established as a supply base and landing point, the earthwork defences were filled in. A triumphal arch was erected in AD85 to commemorate the final conquest of Britain. In the mid-third century, trenches were again dug around the site to protect the monument, and in AD280 stone walls were built to replace them. Remains of these walls, 12ft (3.6m) thick and as high as 24ft (7.2m), can be seen today and they dominate the site; the circle of defensive ditches which surrounded the fortifications can

also be made out. At the centre of the fort is a cruciform platform, all that survives of the Roman monument which was once splendidly encased in marble and decked with bronze statues.

Other remains of several buildings and structures include a first-century cellar, third-century bath house with hypocausts, and the foundations of the chapel of St Augustine. According to a medieval legend, St Augustine landed at Richborough in AD597 on his way to meet Ethelbert, king of Kent, and left his footprint in a stone. The chapel was built in Saxon times to house this saintly relic.

KENT
1½ miles (2.4km) north of Sandwich off A256 OS map 179: ref TR 324602 Open year round; entrance fee payable Wheelchair access Tel: Site office (0304) 612013

ROCHE ABBEY

In a grassy clearing, sheltered by steep wooded cliffs and divided by a stream, stand the ruins of Roche Abbey, as peaceful a retreat today as it was when the abbey was first founded in 1147. The setting, landscaped by 'Capability' Brown in the eighteenth century as part of the grounds of Sandbeck Hall, provides a beautiful backdrop to the substantial ruins of the Cistercian abbey. The walls of the choir of the church are still standing, and excavations have unearthed the complete layout of the monastic buildings, disclosing a particularly good example of abbot's lodgings with hall, kitchen, buttery and other rooms. These are situated beside the infirmary buildings on the south side of the stream.

Roche Abbey was founded by Richard de Bully, Lord of Tickhill, and Richard, son of Turgis, who owned the land on either side of the stream and agreed to become joint founders, allowing the monks to decide where to place the monastery. The monks chose to build on both sides, using the stream as a natural drain, with a dam to control the water supply. The abbey was probably named after a nearby rock which, because of its semblance to a cross, had become a place of pilgrimage. Life at the monastery came to an end in 1538, when it was surrendered to the Crown. Sadly the church and buildings were immediately plundered by local people. According to a contemporary account 'all things of price' were 'either spoiled, carted away, or defaced to the utmost . . . it seemeth that every person bent himself to filch and spoil what he could'.

A small site exhibition provides information on the abbey's history.

SOUTH YORKSHIRE

1½ miles (2.4km) south of Maltby off A634
OS map 111: ref SK 544898
Open during summer months; entrance fee payable
Wheelchair access
Tel: Site office (0709) 812739

ROCHESTER CASTLE

Rising majestically above the river Medway, the massive twelfth-century keep of Rochester Castle still stands at its full height of 113ft (34m) and is one of the finest and best preserved in Britain. There is, however, something rather odd about its corner towers — three are rectangular and one is cylindrical. This is a lasting reminder of the siege of 1215, when King John stormed the castle. One of his main achievements was to destroy the southeastern corner of the keep in a military operation which, in the days before gunpowder, relied on the carcasses of forty pigs: pig fat was used to burn down the wooden pit props of a tunnel beneath the corner tower, which eventually collapsed. It was rebuilt in 1226, in Poitevin style.

The first Norman castle in Rochester was built by Bishop Gundulph for William the Conqueror to defend the Medway crossing. The outer bailey walls followed the line of the old Roman fort. The great keep, which is largely of Kentish ragstone, was added between 1127 and 1139 by William of Corbeil, Archbishop of Canterbury. Although the centre of the keep is now a shell, it is possible to climb the winding stone staircase (427 steps in all) to the battlements, which give beautiful views over the historic city of Rochester and the surrounding countryside. The keep was built on four floors and leading from the central stairway are doorways, smaller staircases and rooms, reminders of the days when it was a lordly luxurious residence.

Charles Dickens spent his childhood in and around Rochester and was particularly fond of the castle: 'A magnificent ruin, what a study for an antiquarian' was the comment of his famous character, Mr Pickwick.

KENT
By Rochester Bridge on A2
OS map 178: ref TQ 742686
Open year round; entrance fee payable
Tel: Site office (0634) 402276

RUSHTON TRIANGULAR LODGE

This extraordinary garden lodge is, as the name suggests, built on a triangular theme. It was the brainchild of Sir Thomas Tresham, a Roman Catholic whose beliefs found no favour in Protestant England in the late sixteenth century, and every feature is symbolic of the Holy Trinity. The three walls form an equilateral triangle, each side having three floors (each with three windows) and three gables rising to three tapering pinnacles. Even the chimney-stack is triangular in shape. And on the same theme, a frieze is carved around the building just below the gables — a continuous inscription with thirty-three letters in each of the three sections.

The exterior is highly ornate and steeped in an overwhelming symbolism. Every architectural detail, emblem and inscription represents the Trinity. The interior, by contrast, is rather plain. The three floors, reached by a spiral staircase, are made up of a hexagonal room with small triangular spaces in each corner. A feature running throughout is the Tresham Coat of Arms, with three trefoils. The extensive use of the Coat of Arms as decoration reminds the visitor of the very personal nature of this eccentric and quite individual building.

The work began on the lodge in 1593, following Tresham's return from prison, where he had been incarcerated for his beliefs. During his imprisonment, Tresham had drawn up plans, notes and sketches of his ideas for the triangular lodge to be built on the grounds of his home, Rushton Hall. The lodge was completed in 1597 and, although it is often thought to be a folly, it was actually called The Warryners Lodge and used by the keeper of rabbits.

NORTHAMPTONSHIRE

1 mile (1.6km) west of Rushton, on unclassified road 3 miles (4.8km) from Desborough on A6
OS map 141: ref SP 830831
Open year round; entrance fee payable
Wheelchair access to grounds only
Tel: Site office (0536) 710761

RYECOTE CHAPEL

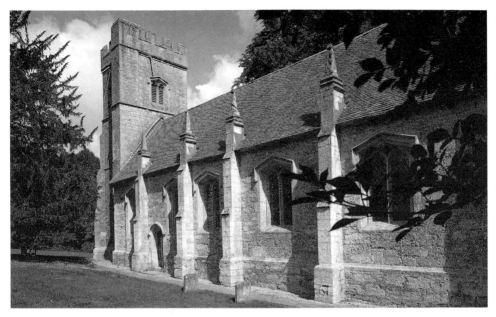

Outside Ryecote Chapel grows a large yew tree which, according to legend, was brought back from the Garden of Gethsemane. This is not necessarily fanciful: the tree is of a type found in Gethsemane, it is certainly very old, and a twelfth-century bishop is recorded as having visited the Holy Land.

Inside the chapel (which is said to be haunted by a grey lady — Cesily Herron, the youngest daughter of Sir Thomas More) truth and legend once again unexpectedly merge. The interior is of outstanding interest because the body of the building, dating from the mid-fifteenth century, is fitted with fine Jacobean carved furniture, screens and panels. The unusual domed pew is said to have been made for Charles I, but recent research has shown that it existed in Elizabethan times. More surprises await visitors who climb the tortuously narrow spiral staircase. Halfway up there is a small room with a fireplace; and up the chimney is an opening with a most extraordinary view looking down the length of the chapel between the roof and the ceiling to a small triangular window. What was its function, no one can be sure.

OXFORDSHIRE

1 mile (1.6km) northeast of M40 (junction 7) and 3 miles
   (4.8km) southwest of Thame off A329
OS map 165: ref SP 667046
Open year round, part week only during winter months;
   entrance fee payable
Wheelchair access to grounds only
Tel: Site office (08447) 346

SAINT AUGUSTINE'S ABBEY

Canterbury is known for its cathedral, a place of pilgrimage, worship and great beauty, but it is also one of the earliest Christian sites in the south of England. It was here that St Augustine and King Ethelbert of Kent established the country's first monastery in AD598, to house Roman monks accompanying Augustine's mission to Britain, which had been ordered by Pope Gregory. The monks followed the simple yet strict rules of the Benedictine order, which laid down a life of prayer, hard work, good deeds and self-discipline, with a set timetable for the day.

The abbey, the oldest Anglo-Saxon abbey in England, became the burial place of St Augustine, the archbishops of Canterbury and the kings of Kent. St Augustine was buried here in AD613, and visitors can see the site of his first tomb. His remains were moved when a new abbey was built soon after the Norman Conquest in 1066, the shrine taking a position above the high altar of the new Romanesque church. It was moved yet again in 1538, at the time of the dissolution of the monasteries, when the abbey was largely demolished; the monks, in reverence to their founder, took the shrine to Chilham.

Enough remains of the abbey, especially of the Norman church with its well-preserved crypt, to give a good idea of the layout. With the magnificent cathedral as backdrop, the ruins make a picturesque and rather haunting sight.

KENT

In Canterbury in Longport ¼ mile (0.4km) east of Cathedral Close
OS map 179: ref TR 154578
Open year round; entrance fee payable
Wheelchair access, assistance required
Tel: Site office (0227) 67345

SAINT BOTOLPH'S PRIORY

The first Augustinian house in England, St Botolph's Priory now stands in ruins, a solemn and beautiful scene in the midst of overgrown trees and weatherbeaten gravestones near the city centre. Until the late eleventh century the Augustinian order was unknown in England, but in 1093 this small community in Colchester decided to adopt the rule and two priests were sent to Normandy to study life in an Augustinian house. They returned with news of the rule and the priory was founded, designed, as was common at the time, to accommodate a prior and twelve priests, symbolizing Christ and his apostles.

Although St Botolph's Priory was granted many privileges and great authority, it was never rich. It was dissolved in 1536 and the building itself was destroyed during the Civil War in a siege of 1648. Unfortunately, nothing now remains of the priory buildings above the ground except the nave of the church. Typically Norman in style, the nave is surrounded by huge columns which support tiers of arches; it is entered by a great west doorway enriched with fine carvings. One of the reasons that the church is so well preserved is that it served as a parish church until 1648. A new church, built in 1836 but designed in Norman style, stands on the southern side of the site.

A feature of the priory ruins often missed by visitors is the bricks of the walls, which still have traces of Roman mortar, showing they were taken from buildings dating back to Roman Colchester.

ESSEX
Colchester, near St Botolph's station OS map 168: ref TL 999249 Open year round; entrance free Wheelchair access Tel: Area office (0223) 358911

SAINT MARY'S CHURCH, KEMPLEY

The beautiful countryside around the village of Kempley, with views over expanses of fertile fields to the Malvern Hills in the distance, is reason enough to visit St Mary's, but the chief attraction of the site is the fascinating and important wall paintings inside the twelfth-century church. They are of two types: tempera (pigments mixed with egg yolk, size or gum, applied to a dry wall) and fresco (the method of painting onto wet plaster with pigments suspended in water). Prominent are frescos of Christ seated on a rainbow, sited at the centre of the ceiling; seraphim surrounded by the sun, moon and stars, in each of the four corners of the vault ceiling; the twelve apostles, on the north and south walls under the arcade; St Peter, on the north wall; and a bishop in full eucharistic vestments, on the east wall. The tempera paintings can be found in the nave. They include the Wheel of Life, on the north wall, and nearby figures of St Anthony of Padua and St Michael.

Of the church building itself, perhaps the most stunning feature is the fourteenth-century half-timbered porch, which all but hides a well-preserved Norman arched doorway. The original church consisted of the present nave and barrel-vaulted chancel. The twelfth-century roof structure survives above the present ceiling, a rare preservation.

Within walking distance is the parish church of Much Marcle. Dating from the thirteenth and fourteenth centuries, it is of great architectural interest and its effigies are said to be some of the finest in the country. The churchyard boasts what is reputed to be the largest and oldest yew tree in England, predating Christianity on this site. Its hollow trunk contains a bench which seats four people.

GLOUCESTERSHIRE

In Kempley 3 miles (4.8km) north of M50 (junction 3) and 6 miles northeast of Ross-on-Wye off A449
OS map 149: ref SO 672296
Admission by appointment with keykeeper
Tel: Area office (0272) 734472

SAINT MARY'S CHURCH, STUDLEY ROYAL

The exterior of St Mary's Church, Studley Royal — broad buttresses, large octagonal pinnacles on the tower, thick tracery bars on the chancel windows together with sculptural decoration, a highly individual porch and abundant Gothic motifs — suggests that it is special. And visitors are rarely disappointed by the exquisite interior which has an elaborate mosaic floor, delicately-coloured marble-clad walls, ornate windows and glowing stained glass.

William Burges, a leading architect in the nineteenth-century Gothic revival, is remembered chiefly for his figurative detail and visual puns, and at Studley Royal he created what has been described as his 'ecclesiastical masterpiece'. Its rich and wide-ranging imagery in sculpture, paint and glass is of outstanding quality. A number of features are especially noteworthy: the sculpture of the annunciation over the entrance porch; scenes from the Virgin's life in the west window; the heads between the chancel windows which represent the conditions of men — a huntsman, peasant, mason, bishop, nobleman, king and queen, knight, monk and, fittingly, architect; brass reliefs on the font showing the ages of man; and the chancel windows which represent the Book of Revelation, a theme which is repeated by the carved angels in the sanctuary roof.

From St Mary's it is possible to see the distant outline of Ripon Cathedral and, in the far distance, the image of a white horse carved into the hillside in the nineteenth century. A pleasant walk leads from St Mary's to the fairytale ruins of Fountains Abbey.

NORTH YORKSHIRE

2½ miles (4km) west of Ripon off B6265 in grounds of Studley Royal estate
OS map 99: ref SE 275693
Open during summer months; entrance free (charge for parking)
Wheelchair access
Tel: Area office (0904) 58626

SAINT MAWES CASTLE

The first impression of St Mawes Castle is that it is exquisite, but quite small. Set in undulating lawned gardens with attractive flowerbeds and a water garden, it has a picture-book quality. But along with its counterpart, Pendennis Castle across the inlet, St Mawes was an important link in Henry VIII's coastal defences and a serious fortress. Yet, although it was a formidable barrier against attack from the sea, from the landward side, its position on a hill slope made it impossible to defend. This became apparent at the time of the Civil War, when the castle was a royalist garrison. It capitulated to General Fairfax in 1646 without, apparently, a single shot being fired.

Today's visitor is immediately aware of the castle's balanced shamrock shape: the central round keep is surrounded by three semicircular bastions. Compact as a warship, St Mawes is an excellent place to display the cannon which once defended the coastal waters. Especially interesting is the Sigismondo Alberghetti — a cannon of this type could fire heavy shot up to a range of 2000 yards (1829m). More cannon can be found perched above the secluded beach which may be reached from the castle's grounds.

CORNWALL
In St Mawes on A3078 OS map 204: ref SW 842328 Open year round; entrance fee payable Wheelchair access to grounds and ground floor only Tel: Site office (0326) 270526

SAINT PAUL'S MONASTERY, JARROW

On this lovely spot overlooking the river Don, St Benedict Biscop founded St Paul's Monastery in AD685. St Paul's gained an international reputation — this was where singing of the plainsong office was introduced and where the beautifully illustrated Bible *Codex Amiatinus*, was scribed. Above all, the monastery has become famous as the home of the Venerable Bede, the greatest European scholar of the eighth century. Bede wrote many learned books from his monastery cell, including his *History of the English Church and People*. He also brought to England the idea of dating years from the birth of Christ and wrote the first English translation of the Gospel of St John.

The site is now dominated by the remains of the Norman monastery built c. 1075, but the plan of the Saxon monastery can still be seen. The existing parish church, which stands beside the ruins, contains many fragments of the historic monastery. The original chapel survives as the chancel and the exquisitely carved Dedication Stone, dated 23 April AD685, is in the north porch. There is also an ancient chair which is believed to have belonged to Bede.

Nearby in Jarrow Hall, the Bede Monastery Museum has exhibits tracing the history of St Paul's Monastery and the life and works of the Venerable Bede.

TYNE & WEAR

In Jarrow, on minor road north of A185
OS map 88: ref NZ 339652
Open year round; entrance free
Wheelchair access
Tel: Area office (0228) 31777

SAXTEAD GREEN MILL

The post-mills of east Suffolk were the finest of their type in England, and Saxtead Green Mill, which stopped work in 1947, is an excellent and well-preserved example. The body or 'buck' of the mill rotates on an upright post, hence the term 'post-mill'. The buck, a wooden superstructure set on a brick roundhouse, contains the machinery and carries the four sails. It is turned by the 'fantail', or 'fly', at the rear so that the sails face square into the 'eye of the wind'.

The present white-painted mill dates back to at least 1796, when records show that it was worked by Mr Amos Webber. There has been, however, a mill on the site for more than 650 years; a survey of 1309 reported that the spindles and mill-stones were in good condition. The last miller at Saxstead was the late Steve Aldred; his hat still hangs on its peg and his mill is in perfect working order, as at the final milling in 1947.

The mill stands an impressive 46ft (14m) high with a sail-span of some 55ft (16.7m), and its workings may be understood by an examination of the interior; a diagram on the ground floor of the roundhouse helps explain the different components and the milling process.

There are three floors to the roundhouse, used for delivery of the sacks of grain and for storage. The cat-flap in the door was an essential feature of the building: one rat or mouse could cause havoc! A steep wooden ladder at the tail of the mill leads to the buck, where the mill-stones and machinery, an ingenious display of precision, balance and harmony, can be examined.

SUFFOLK
2½ miles (4km) northwest of Framlingham on A1120 OS map 156: ref TM 253645 Open during summer months; entrance fee payable Wheelchair access to exterior only Tel: Site office (0728) 82789

SHERBORNE OLD CASTLE

Sherborne Old Castle was built in the early twelfth century by Roger de Caen, Bishop of Salisbury and the greatest landowner in the region. Its most famous occupant was Sir Walter Ralegh, who was granted the lease by Queen Elizabeth I in 1592: Ralegh loved Sherborne, which he described as his 'fortune's fold', and to understand why, visitors need only to take a short walk around this beautiful town, which was named by the Saxons 'scir burne', meaning 'the place of the clear stream'. Of outstanding merit is the church of St Mary the Virgin, which is famed for its splendid fan vaulting (the earliest of this type to have been been built) and is one of the most attractive surviving examples of the Perpendicular style. The south range of the medieval castle, which stands on rising ground, was demolished by Ralegh, thus opening the view to the south from the courtyard. Ralegh was also responsible for the enlargement of Sherborne Lodge (now known as Sherborne Castle) which stands in pretty parkland beside a fine lake.

The dilapidated state of the old castle is the result of the Civil War. Lord Digby, one of Charles I's principal advisors, held it for the sovereign in 1642 and again in 1645. In the latter year parliamentary forces under General Fairfax laid full-scale siege to the castle, which Oliver Cromwell described as a 'malicious and mischievous castle like its owner'. The besieged garrison, under Digby's step-son, Sir Lewis Dyve, surrendered after sixteen days. Parliament ordered the defences to be dismantled and the castle was left a ruin. Its crumbling stones, which glow a mellow, golden shade, now offer only glimpses of its earlier striking proportions. A curtain wall and bastion earthwork surround the remains of the courtyard and hall range, making the distinctive eight-sided symmetrical shape. But the most impressive of the surviving buildings is the southwest gatehouse; ashlar-faced and full height in the northwest corner, it points like a large index finger into the sky.

DORSET
½ mile (0.8km) east of Sherborne on north side of lake OS map 183: ref ST 647167 Open year round; entrance fee payable Wheelchair access Tel: Site office (093581) 2730

SIBSEY TRADER WINDMILL

Once renowned for its fertile corn-growing land, Lincolnshire had many mills dotted around the countryside. One of the finest still standing is Sibsey Trader, a six-sailed tower mill named after the nearby village of Sibsey, where the bricks were made, and the river Trader, along which barges carried the grain to be ground. The mill was built in 1877 and follows a style typical in the county, with a tapering brick-built tower tarred outside and whitewashed inside, and topped by a white-painted cap which supports the sails, each with a span of more than 60ft (18.2m). As a tower mill, the main body stands firm and only the cap turns in the wind.

The mill stopped work in the late 1950s, but the machinery has been beautifully maintained and is still in good working order. Visitors can climb wooden ladders to the six floors, each diminishing in size, and follow the whole milling process with the help of informative interpretive displays.

LINCOLNSHIRE
½ mile (0.8km) west of village of Sibsey, off A16 5 miles (8km) north of Boston
OS map 122: ref TF 345511
Open during summer months, part week only; entrance fee payable
Wheelchair access to exterior and grounds only
Tel: Site office (0205) 750036

STANTON DREW CIRCLES AND COVE

Tucked away just east of the tiny village of Stanton Drew is a group of stone circles which, although less well-known than Stonehenge or Avebury, is widely considered to be one of the finest Bronze Age monuments of its type. It consists of three stone circles, two of which have avenues of standing stones extending from them. A short walk away, in the garden of the village public house, The Druids' Arms, is a 'cove', thought to be a burial chamber. There are many traditions surrounding the stones, of which perhaps the most romantic legend is that they represent a wedding party turned into stone as punishment for their over-zealous merrymaking. According to an account of 1743, by the famous antiquary John Stukeley:

This noble monument is vulgarly call'd the Weddings; and they say 'tis a company that assisted at a nuptial solemnity thus petrify'd. In an orchard near the church is a cove consisting of three stones . . . this they call'd the parson, the bride and the bridegroom. Other circles are said to be the company dancing; and a separate parcel of stones standing a little from the rest are call'd the fiddlers, or the band of musick.

AVON

Circles: east of Stanton Drew village off B3130
Cove: in Stanton Drew, in garden of Druid's Arms
OS map 172: Circles ref ST 601634; Cove ref ST 598633
Open year round; entrance fee at discretion of landowner
Tel: Area office (0272) 734472

STOKESAY CASTLE

Local folklore has it that two giant brothers once lived on the hill tops overlooking Stokesay Castle; one lived on View Edge, the other on Norton Camp. The brothers kept their money in a chest under Stokesay, and would throw the key to each other between the two summits. One day the key fell short and dropped into the pool beside Stokesay: the key and chest were lost forever, but it is said that a raven still guards them both.

Stokesay is an early thirteenth-century fortified house, the oldest and best-preserved which survives in England. It has a most romantic setting. The attractive huddle of buildings (gatehouse, south tower, north tower, solar and great hall) and pretty walled courtyard, surrounded by a moat, are set in gentle Shropshire countryside. Yet the tranquillity of Stokesay today is very different from what must have been its atmosphere in the Middle Ages. A high wall around the courtyard, fragments of which can still be seen, would have produced a dark, claustrophobic effect. Where now there are lawns and flower-filled spaces, there was a clutter of buildings — kitchens and a buttery are known to have adjoined the north tower and other buildings once existed in front of the solar block and south tower. The oldest surviving part of the structure is the lower part of the north block, which dates from c.1240; much of the rest dates from 1280

when Lawrence Ludlow, one of the richest wool merchants of his day, bought and rebuilt Stokesay, fortifying it under licence from King Edward I. Lawrence's addition of an extra top floor to the north tower created perhaps the most picturesque aspect of Stokesay; it houses a fine medieval fireplace. But the most impressive of all his additions is the magnificent, spacious hall, which was the hub of the manor's activities. Here the lord and his family, guests and servants took their meals; the court was also held here, and servants bedded down for the night on the floor of the hall. It must have been a draughty place, for only the upper windows were glazed, the lower ones being merely shuttered, as they are seen today. Beside the great hall is the solar, the private chamber to which the lord and his family withdrew. Its present fittings, which date from the seventeenth century, include panelling and two peepholes which look down onto the hall below. The delightfully decorated gatehouse, an Elizabethan addition to Stokesay, is the only part of the site still inhabited.

SHROPSHIRE

1 mile (1.6km) south of Craven Arms off A49
OS map 137: ref SO 436817
Open spring to autumn; entrance fee payable
Wheelchair access to gardens and great hall only
Tel: Site office (05882) 2544

STOTT PARK BOBBIN MILL

Now a thriving industrial heritage monument, Stott Park Bobbin Mill was once the workplace for some sixty men, women and children, many of whom lived in the nearby small cottages. Its main product, the bobbins, had a ready market in the north of England where the textile trade rapidly expanded during the nineteenth and early twentieth centuries. But although Stott Park made a wide variety of bobbins for both industrial and domestic use, it also produced a number of other goods. Order books for 1908-16 include such items as axe-shafts, pea sticks, file handles, spade crowns, toggles, milk-can handles and bill-hook handles.

Conditions inside the mill were typical of the nineteenth-century workplace; child labour, dangerous machinery, long working days and dust-polluted air were the norm. The museum today is necessarily a cleaner and safer place to visit than the mill known to Charles Jackson, who is recorded in the 1841 census as an apprentice (aged fifteen) at the mill. He is known to have married a local woman, Anne Fell, and to have had six children, four of whom died in infancy. Jackson's eldest son followed his father into the mill and became a bobbin turner.

Visitors to the museum can see the process of bobbin turning, along with cutting, boring, roughing, drying, finishing and polishing. All the original machinery of the mill has been preserved in full working order.

CUMBRIA

½ mile (0.8km) north of Finsthwaite near Newby Bridge
OS map 96: ref SD 373883
Open during summer months; entrance fee payable
Wheelchair access to ground floor only
Tel: Site office (0448) 31087

THETFORD PRIORY

The Priory of Our Lady at Thetford, where the statue of the Virgin Mary was credited with miraculous powers of healing, was once a place of pilgrimage. A large Lady Chapel was built in the early thirteenth century to house the statue and the remains of this, including the spiral staircase leading to a small room where a monk stood watch over the visiting pilgrims, can still be seen.

The priory, which belonged to the order of Cluny, was founded in 1103-4 by Roger Bigod, friend of William the Conquerer. In the fifteenth century it achieved fame as the burial place for the Howard Dukes of Norfolk. The magnificent tombs were transferred from the priory church to Framlingham in Suffolk at the dissolution of the monasteries. Although the priory is now in ruins, the site gives a good indication of the layout of the monastic buildings, including the little cloister of the monks' infirmary with its cobbled paving (a few cobbles survive). The magnificent fourteenth-century three-storeyed gatehouse is also accessible to visitors. Two miles (3.2km) away are the ruins of Thetford Warren Lodge, thought to have been the home of the prior's gamekeeper.

Thetford, now a quiet country town, was the seat of East Anglian bishops until 1901, and there were no fewer than twelve churches and four monastic houses there by the reign of Edward III. The town lost its importance after the dissolution of the monasteries, but three medieval churches are intact and, as well as the substantial remains of Thetford Priory, there are ruins of two other monastic houses, the Benedictine Nunnery of St George and the Augustinian Priory of the Holy Sepulchre.

NORFOLK

On the west side of Thetford off A11
OS map 144: ref TL 865836
Open year round; entrance free
Wheelchair access
Tel: Area office (0223) 358911

Thetford Warren Lodge
2 miles (3.2km) west of Thetford off B1107
OS map 144: ref TL 839841
Open year round; entrance free

Church of the Holy Sepulchre
On the west side of Thetford off B1107
OS map 144: ref TL 865831
Open year round
Wheelchair access, assistance required

TITCHFIELD ABBEY

The imposing ruins of Titchfield Abbey, later known as Place House, are a source of many tales, some tall, some true. One of the most bizarre is a story that the fishpond once overflowed and nearly drowned Richard II; another tells that Margaret of Anjou was presented with a live lion on the occasion of her marriage to Henry VI at the abbey. Certainly, Charles I spent his last night of freedom here, and it is thought that the abbey was the stage for the debut of some of Shakespeare's courtly plays.

Titchfield Abbey was founded in 1232 by Peter des Roches, Bishop of Winchester, for Premonstratensian canons, the last house of that order to be established in England. It was dissolved in 1537, when it passed to Thomas Wriothesley, later first Earl of Southampton, a powerful subordinate to Thomas Cromwell and supreme influence in the dissolution of the monasteries. He began remodelling the buildings, converting the nave of the church and a section of the cloistral buildings into a private mansion, known as Place House. As the contemporary antiquary, John Leland, wrote: 'Mr Wriothesley hath builded a right stately house embateled and having a goodely gate and a conduct [conduit] casteled in the middle of the court of it, yn the very same place where the late Monasterie of Premonstratenses stoode, callyd Titchfelde.'

The house, a family home for over two centuries, was largely demolished in 1781, but the 'goodely gate' remains, a Gothic-style gatehouse with gargoyles on the parapets and imitation arrow-slit windows, which was converted from the nave of the church. Fragments of other walls also survive. The outline of the original abbey buildings, including some of the cloister decorated with fine thirteenth-century floor tiles, can be identified.

The nearby parish Church of St Peter in Titchfield village belonged to the abbey until the dissolution. The church is particularly noted for the magnificent marble and alabaster memorial monument to Thomas Wriothesley.

HAMPSHIRE
½ mile (0.8km) north of Titchfield off A27 OS map 196: ref SU 539065 Open during summer months; entrance fee payable Wheelchair access Tel: Site office (0329) 43016

TYNEMOUTH PRIORY AND CASTLE

A fourteenth-century gateway frames the magnificent Norman priory church and leads visitors into the ruins of Tynemouth Priory and Castle, standing on the headland which forms the north side of the mouth of the Tyne. The weathered graveslabs, some dating back to the seventeenth century, are testimony to harsh conditions, but the views over the Tyne estuary and along the coastline are breathtaking.

The priory was founded in the seventh century and became an important monastic house after the murdered St Oswin was buried there in AD651. Stories of miracles at his shrine brought wealth and fame and the monastery became a place of pilgrimage. It fell to the Danes in the mid-ninth century, however, and the church and buildings were plundered and destroyed. The nuns of St Hilda's who had taken shelter there were all massacred. The abandoned monastery was re-established as a Benedictine priory for the monks from St Albans Abbey in 1090. Well-endowed and prosperous, it continued as a favourite burial spot and in 1127 the body of St Henry of Coquet, who had lived alone in a cell on the island of Coquet, was buried near the shrine of St Oswin. Outstanding among the remains are the two walls of the presbytery which still stand at their full height and the fifteenth-century Percy Chantry

chapel with its superb collection of roof bosses.

The site of the priory was of such military significance for the defence of the mouth of the Tyne that from the thirteenth century onwards it was fortified. Tynemouth Castle consisted of a gatehouse with a barbican and curtain walls which enclosed the priory buildings. A new gatehouse was built in the fourteenth century to replace the original one and it proved so effective a bulwark in the border wars between Northumbria and Scotland that after the dissolution of the monasteries Henry VIII decided to retain the priory as a royal castle and fortress.

An artillery battery was installed here at the end of the nineteenth century and was operational until after World War II. In 1904 three magazines were built, one of which has been restored to its original condition (lit with candle-lamps). It now contains a fascinating exhibition of equipment, photographs and clothing.

TYNE & WEAR

In Tynemouth, near North Pier
OS map 88: ref NZ 374695
Open year round, part week only during winter months; entrance fee payable
Wheelchair access to castle only
Tel: Site office (0632) 571090

UPNOR CASTLE

Upnor Castle makes an attractive sight with its turreted facade, especially when viewed from the river, but it has a most undistinguished history as a fortification. Built between 1560 and 1563 by Elizabeth I to protect the fleet and the new dockyard at Chatham, it failed in the task. The castle, which consisted of a large angle bastion, or gun platform, facing the river, and a residential block, was one of a chain protecting the Medway. It was enlarged and strengthened in 1599-1601, but in 1667, when a Dutch fleet under de Ruyter sailed up the river, despite spirited resistance the castle did not deter the raiders: only half the guns on the bastion could be brought into action at one time against the approaching ships.

Replaced by a newer fort down river, Upnor

Castle was converted into a magazine for gunpowder and munitions, a use which proved much more suitable. Indeed, in 1691, Upnor had the greatest store of gunpowder in England. Replica powder barrels, built to hold as much as 100lb (45.5kg) of gunpowder, are on show in the castle, and on the top floor there are fascinating displays on the history of the Medway fortifications.

KENT
At Upnor on unclassified road off A228
OS map 178: ref TQ 758706
Open during summer months; entrance fee payable
Wheelchair access to grounds only
Tel: Site office (0634) 718742

WALMER CASTLE

William Pitt the Younger lived here, the Duke of Wellington died here, and Queen Victoria paid a visit lasting nearly a month. Walmer Castle has played host to many famous and distinguished public figures, relics of whom are displayed inside, making it an interesting and unusual museum. The rooms are furnished with fine pieces of period furniture and contain a great variety of memorabilia, chiefly devoted to Wellington, who was particulary fond of Walmer. There are his telescope and folding camp chair, his death mask, and the wing chair in which he died at the age of eighty-three — and, of course, a pair of the famous 'Wellington boots'.

Walmer Castle, an artillery fort, was built 1539-40 by Henry VIII as one of the 'castles which keep the Downs'. Powerful and formidable, the castle is enclosed within a broad, deep moat and consists of a circular central keep with four large rounded bastions projecting from it. The castle, which saw action only in the Civil War, has been the official residence of the Lords Warden of the Cinque Ports since the early eighteenth century. The office was developed in the thirteenth century and gave the holder authority over the five ports (Hastings, Romney, Hythe, Dover and Sandwich) responsible for providing ships in time of danger. Among past Lord Wardens have been such celebrated figures as Viscount Palmerston, Lord Granville, W.H. Smith, of the famous booksellers, and Sir Winston Churchill.

Although some chose not to live at Walmer, many did, and made the alterations and improvements you can see today. Lord Granville did much to convert it from a fortress into a home, during his term of office in the second half of the nineteenth century. He built thirteen extra rooms, and laid out much of the gardens.

The extensive gardens are a special feature, delightfully landscaped with colourful herbaceous borders and an abundance of carefully chosen trees and shrubs. They were first planned by Lady Hester Stanhope while she was staying with William Pitt during his office (1792-1806). She wrote: 'I am not dull, or, rather, not idle, as I have the charge of improvements here — plantations, farm buildings etc.', and the results of her efforts, and those of later occupants, are here for everyone to enjoy.

KENT

On B2057, coast road south of Walmer
OS map 179: ref TR 378501
Open year round, part week only; closed when Lord Warden in residence; entrance fee payable
Wheelchair access to courtyard and gardens only
Tel: Site office (0304) 364288

WARKWORTH HERMITAGE

Just half a mile from Warkworth Castle, with its magnificent fifteenth-century keep, is a far less imposing but equally impressive sight, Warkworth Hermitage, a fourteenth-century cell and chapel carved out of the hard rock of the left bank of the river Coquet. Hidden by trees and approached by an attractive footpath and then by ferry, the hermitage abounds with romantic legends.

A favourite story recounts the sad and lonely penitence of a northern knight, Sir Robert of Bothal. According to legend Sir Robert fell in love with the beautiful Lady Isabel Widdrington, but before she would agree to marry him she wanted proof of his valour. He joined an expedition against the Scots and was wounded in action. Hearing the news, Lady Isabel rushed to his aid and was captured by the Scots on the way. She escaped with the help of her brother only to encounter Sir Robert who, mistaking her rescuer for a rival, stabbed both him and Lady Isabel. As a penance, the tragic Sir Robert carved out this quiet hideaway in the grounds of the castle.

Very little is actually known about the foundation of the hermitage, which is first mentioned in records of 1487, when Thomas Barker was appointed by the fourth Earl of Northumberland as the first in a line of hermits who lived in it until the mid-sixteenth century.

The hermitage was remarkably sophisticated for its time — its three rooms (a chapel, a confessional and a cell) making it quite unlike the many roughly hewn caverns found around the country. Today, the hermit's lodgings are in ruins, but the chapel, dedicated to the Holy Trinity, is in good condition. It contains several curious sculptures, notably a stone effigy of a reclining lady with a man kneeling beside her, his head resting on one hand, the other clasped to his head in grief. One theory suggests this may be a Nativity, but others prefer the supposition that the reclining lady is Lady Isabel, with Sir Robert by her side. Many people even go so far as to say that perhaps the inscription carved in the chapel walls and still visible '*Fuerunt mihi lacrymae panes die ac nocte*' ('my tears have been my meat, by day and by night') was the painstaking work of Sir Robert during his lonely life here.

NORTHUMBERLAND

7½ miles (12km) south of Alnwick on A1068; access by ferry from below Warkworth Castle
OS map 81: ref NU 242060
Open during summer months, weekends only; entrance fee payable
Tel: Site office (0665) 711423

WENLOCK PRIORY

If you have an interest in drama, try to visit Wenlock Priory when it is hosting an open-air theatre production (usually Shakespeare). A stage is erected in front of the chapterhouse, and the whole of this ancient ruined priory is beautifully and atmospherically floodlit.

A monastery was founded at Wenlock c. AD690 by Merewald, a member of the royal house of the kingdom of Mercia. Some time after the Norman Conquest, it was refounded as a Cluniac priory. The order put great emphasis on elaborate ritual performed in the finest vestments, and Wenlock Priory was intended to be a magnificent edifice to God. In 1101, while building was in progress, bones believed to be those of St Milburga were found, and Wenlock soon became a place of pilgrimage. By the mid-twelfth century, a small town had developed around the increasingly prosperous priory. A great Norman church was built to replace an early Saxon building, and monks were sent out to new priories at Paisley, Dudley, St Helen's (Isle of Wight) and Church Preen. As expansion continued, the Norman church was replaced by a larger one. Its timber was

a gift from King Henry III: the Crown held a right of hospitality at the priory and the king exercised this right on several occasions — he even had his favourite wine sent from Bristol and stored for his own use.

Today's visitors find plenty to explore: the remains of the priory church, 350ft (106.6m) long; the cloisters, which once formed the main place of work for the monks, who used the area for study, writing books, and teaching novices; and the Norman chapterhouse, whose exuberantly interlaced decorative arcading is typical Cluniac work. Many visitors comment on the attractive house within the priory precinct. It was built at the end of the fifteenth century for Prior Richard and survived the dissolution of the monasteries remarkably intact. It is now privately occupied.

SHROPSHIRE

In Much Wenlock, off B4376
OS map 127: ref SJ 625001
Open year round part week only during winter months
Wheelchair access, assistance required
Tel: Site office (0952) 727466

THE WINE MERCHANT'S HOUSE, SOUTHAMPTON

The smell of wood smoke pervades this medieval merchant's house, just as it did in the fourteenth century, when some sixty buildings of this type existed in Southampton, and visitors can purchase wine, cider, beer and spices just as the medieval customers once bought their wares. The shop is a reconstruction, but the main hall, the centre of the house, is substantially unaltered since the fourteenth century. In this large room (it occupies about a third of the building and is open to the roof) the merchant conducted his more public transactions, while in the nearby and much smaller inner room, which perhaps served as a counting house, he went about his important private business. On the first floor are two chambers and the eastern one deserves a particularly careful look, for it appears today much as it did when the house was first built. The floor is of interest — the oak boards are laid in rebates cut into the floor joists.

Situated near Southampton's dock, French Street is in an historic part of the city and nearby there are many interesting buildings and museums: God's House Tower (Winkle Street), a museum which traces Southampton's past from prehistoric times to the Middle Ages; Tudor House (St Michael's Square), a building with a twelfth-century timbered facade which contains items relating to the city's social history; Southampton Maritime Museum (Town Quay) housed in a medieval woolhouse; and The Bargate Museum (The Bargate), housed in the chamber above the twelfth-century gateway which controlled access to Southampton from the north.

HAMPSHIRE

In French Street (no. 58), between Castle Way and Town Quay
OS map 196: ref SU 419112
Open during summer months; entrance fee payable
Tel: Area office (0892) 48166

WITLEY COURT

Only the burnt-out shell of Witley Court survives, yet even the ruins of this baroque-style country house convey the magnificence of a vanished age. The architect, Samuel Dankes, building around an earlier house during the 1860s for Lord Ward, was responsible for the remains which can be seen today. Mounting the elegant flight of steps leading to a large portico (by Nash), visitors can immediately sense the former opulence of Witley Court; and on passing through the decaying inner walls and emerging on the garden side, its true splendour is appreciated. To the right is a pavilion and an orangery, while directly ahead is the most memorable image of Witley, the colossal Perseus fountain, which rises 26ft (7.9m) above the water. Photographs of the fountain in action can be seen in the adjacent Great Witley Parish Church.

Glowing gold and white and suffused with light, the church is itself a small masterpiece. It was built in the 1730s for the first Lord Foley and the ceiling paintings by Antonio Belluci (two large and twenty small pieces set into papier maché worked to look like stucco) were purchased by the second Lord Foley in 1747 from the palace of the Duke of Chandos. Both court and church are set in the vestiges of a grand formal garden laid out by W. E Nesfield in the late nineteenth century. Belvederes flank the central fountain, but the flower beds are now mere memories overwhelmed by acres of lawn. Witley Court's memories are of a lost world of poised promenades, parasol-shaded teas, and elegant dances.

HEREFORD & WORCESTER

10 miles (16km) northwest of Worcester on A443
OS map 150: ref SO 769649
Open year round; entrance free
Tel: Area office (0902) 765105

WOLVESEY OLD BISHOP'S PALACE

Winchester was the wealthiest and most influential bishopric in England during the Middle Ages and the Norman palace was a suitably grand and luxurious residence for the bishops, who held positions of great importance in both Church and State. Although the old palace is now in ruins (the new residence was built just to the south of it in the 1680s), the remains of Wolvesey, standing in the shadow of the cathedral, conjure up a picture of what was once a magnificent and powerful building.

The palace, one of the greatest and most elaborate houses of the time, was largely the work of two bishops, William Giffard, bishop from 1107 to 1129, and Henry of Blois (in office from 1129 to 1171), grandson of William the Conqueror and brother of King Stephen. Giffard built what is now the west hall, and Henry was responsible for the east hall; these two large buildings were sited on a central courtyard. During the civil wars of King Stephen's reign, it became necessary for Henry to add fortifications; the east hall was transformed by the addition of a strong fortified tower (later known as Wymond's Tower) in the southeast corner, and a large 'keep' at the east end. Other

major works, such as defensive walls to enclose the palace, which was then probably also moated for the first time, meant that Henry's original 'house like a palace' became fortified 'like a castle'.

The old palace survived for five centuries virtually unaltered, prestigious and popular with royalty. It became costly and inconvenient, however, and in the 1680s Bishop Morley built a new house in the Baroque style, the west wing of which is the present bishops' palace.

The entrance to the ruins of Wolvesey is on College Street, one of the loveliest streets in Winchester (on which stands the house where novelist Jane Austen died), and can be reached by one of two picturesque routes; either via the Weirs, a pretty riverside walk, or from the cathedral through Cathedral Close, then via King's Gate to College Street.

HAMPSHIRE

¼ mile (0.4km) south of Winchester Cathedral, next to the
 Bishop's Palace, access from College Street
OS map 185: ref SU 484291
Open during summer months; entrance fee payable
Wheelchair access
Tel: Site office (0962) 54766

WREST PARK HOUSE AND GARDENS

Wrest Park House is itself impressive, but the beautifully landscaped gardens, surrounded by water, are the really arresting feature of the Wrest Park estate. Set just east of the Bedfordshire village of Silsoe, the estate belonged to the de Grey family, first Earls, then Dukes of Kent, from c.1280 to 1859 and the family took great pride and pleasure in the grounds. Laid out in the first half of the eighteenth century, the gardens are extensive and varied, showing examples of different styles of design at the time. The finest of the gardens is the semi-formal Great Garden, laid out by the first Duke of Kent and later modified by 'Capability' Brown. A myriad of fascinating alleyways, hidden clearings and superb vistas of buildings and monuments provide something to catch the eye at every turn, including the dogs' cemetery (where Tottie, Little Dick and other favourite pets are buried), the Palladian Bowling Green House, and the Pavilion, designed by Thomas Archer in 1709-11. Other interesting and unusual features include the orangery (now a tea-room), the Bath House, Cascade Bridge, a folly built as a ruin, and the French Garden, with a marble fountain and laurel-lined avenues.

The house, built to replace the Tudor house which stood on the site of what is now the French Garden, was designed in the French style in 1834-39 by the second Earl de Grey, the first president of the Royal Institute of British Architects. Several of the rooms are open to the public and they contain some fine plasterwork, especially the ceiling of the dining room, which is decorated with the 'joys of the table' — fowl, fruit, flesh and fish. The entrance hall, which is dominated by the great staircase, is lined with portraits of the de Grey family, royalty and distinguished notables.

Nearby, in the village of Flitton, is the mausoleum of the de Grey family, which contains a superb collection of monuments dating from the sixteenth century to the nineteenth.

BEDFORDSHIRE

¾ mile (1.2km) east of Silsoe off A6
OS map 153: ref TL 093356
Open during summer months, weekends only; entrance fee payable
Wheelchair access, assistance required
Tel: Site office (0525) 60718

De Grey Mausoleum

In Flitton, attached to church, on unclassified road ¾ mile (1.2km) south of A507, 1½ miles (2.4km) west of A6 at Silsoe
OS map 153: ref TL 059359
Open year round; access through keykeeper
Wheelchair access, assistance required
Tel: Area office (0223) 358911

WROXETER ROMAN CITY

The Roman settlement of Viroconium was established here as early as AD58. It is believed to have been a legionary occupation under Veranius, a young commander sent by Nero to deal with the turbulent Welsh. Later, when the site was handed over to civil authorities, a thriving city developed and traders from as far away as Gaul and Germany established shops in which to sell their wares. It was visited by Hadrian in AD120 or 121, and at this time public buildings were erected on a huge scale, including the impressive baths complex which can be viewed today. The north wall of the frigidarium survives and helps to provide the scale of the other remains which form the plan of the bath house. The outlines of the frigidarium, tepidarium, laconica and caldarium can be made out. These, as the names suggest, were a succession of bathing rooms graduating from cold to very hot — a laconicum was a sauna-type hot, dry room and the caldarium, the alternative final stage, contained scalding hot plunge baths.

The Romans demolished, rebuilt and extended buildings as necessary and some of the most interesting archaeological work recently undertaken is aimed at discovering when and how these changes took place. A visit to the site museum provides visitors with a good insight into present theories, together with a selection of 'evidence' — pottery, coins, and a fascinating array of objects — found on the site.

A short and very pleasant stroll down the nearby lane (walking towards the prominent conical landmarks of Caer-caradoc and Lawley hills) will bring you to Saxon-built Wroxeter church. It was constructed in part with stone from the Roman town — the gateposts, for instance, are a pair of fine Roman pillars. The return walk also provides possibly the most attractive view of the silhouetted frigidarium wall.

SHROPSHIRE

At Wroxeter, 5 miles (8km) east of Shrewsbury, 1 mile (1.6km) off A5
OS map 126: ref SJ 568088
Open year round; entrance fee payable
Wheelchair access, except to viewing platform
Tel: Site office (074375) 330

YARMOUTH CASTLE

The harbour town of Yarmouth provides a lovely setting for Yarmouth Castle, the last of the string of castles commissioned by Henry VIII for coastal defence. It has changed a lot since it was built *c.*1549; the moat was filled in and a house, now the George Hotel, was built over it by Sir Robert Holmes, Captain of the Island, in the late seventeenth century. As part of his grand reorganization of the castle, Holmes also had much of the earthworks demolished, the gatehouse blocked and a new entrance built on the south side. However, although much reduced in size — it is essentially a square with sides about 100ft (30.4m) long — Yarmouth Castle retains its most distinctive feature: a sharply pointed bastion, one of the earliest of its kind in England. Called 'arrow-head' because of their shape, these bastions were at that time the latest thinking in military architecture, giving total protection with

minimum exposure and replacing the old-fashioned, low, round bastions.

There were plans for a complete modernization of the castle in the mid-nineteenth century, but they were never implemented and the small garrison was eventually withdrawn in 1885; the castle then served as a signalling post until 1901. Although used by the military during the two World Wars it has now been well restored, and there is an excellent exhibition on the history of the castle and the part it played in the overall development of coastal defence under Henry VIII.

ISLE OF WIGHT

In Yarmouth adjacent to car ferry terminal
OS map 196: ref SZ 354898
Open during summer months; entrance fee payable
Wheelchair access to ground floor only
Tel: Site office (0983) 760678

SITE SELECTOR

ANCIENT SITES

Castlerigg Stone Circle, *Cumbria*

Grimes Graves, *Norfolk*

Old Sarum, *Wiltshire*

ROMAN SITES

Aldborough Roman Town, *North Yorkshire*

Lullingstone Roman Villa, *Kent*

North Leigh Roman Villa, *Oxfordshire*

Portchester Castle, *Hampshire*

Richborough Castle, *Kent*

Wroxeter Roman City, *Shropshire*

RECOMMENDED FOR A RAINY DAY

Aydon Castle, *Northumberland*

Berwick Barracks, *Northumberland*

Bolsover Castle, *Derbyshire*

Boscobel House, *Shropshire*

Gainsborough Old Hall, *Lincolnshire*

Goodshaw Chapel, *Lancashire*

Longthorpe Tower, *Cambridgeshire*

Lyddington Bede House, *Leicestershire*

Marble Hill House, *Greater London*

Old Merchant's House and Row 111 Houses,
Great Yarmouth, *Norfolk*

Prior's Hall Barn, Widdington, *Essex*

Ryecote Chapel, *Oxfordshire*

St Mary's Church, Kempley, *Gloucestershire*

St Mary's Church, Studley Royal,
North Yorkshire

Stokesay Castle, *Shropshire*

Stott Park Bobbin Mill, *Cumbria*

Walmer Castle, *Kent*

Wine Merchant's House, Southampton,
Hampshire

SITES SUITABLE FOR PICNICKING

Acton Burnell Castle, *Shropshire*

Appuldurcombe House, *Isle of Wight*

Barnard Castle, *Durham*

Belsay Hall, Castle and Gardens,
Northumberland

Bishop's Waltham Palace, *Hampshire*

Castlerigg Stone Circle, *Cumbria*

Castle Rising Castle, *Norfolk*

Egglestone Abbey, *Durham*

Goodrich Castle, *Hereford & Worcester*

Hurst Castle, *Hampshire*

Marble Hill House, *Greater London*

Minster Lovell Hall, *Oxfordshire*

Mount Grace Priory, *North Yorkshire*

Netley Abbey, *Hampshire*

Okehampton Castle, *Devon*

Old Sarum, *Dorset*

Pickering Castle, *North Yorkshire*

Roche Abbey, *South Yorkshire*

St Mary's Church, Kempley, *Gloucestershire*

St Mawes Castle, *Cornwall*

Stokesay Castle, *Shropshire*

Walmer Castle, *Kent*

Warkworth Hermitage, *Northumberland*

Wenlock Priory, *Shropshire*

Witley Court, *Hereford & Worcester*

Wrest Park House and Gardens, *Bedfordshire*

MEDIEVAL CASTLES AND LATER FORTIFICATIONS

Acton Burnell Castle, *Shropshire*

Ashby de la Zouch Castle, *Leicestershire*

Aydon Castle, *Northumberland*

Baconsthorpe Castle, *Norfolk*

Barnard Castle, *Durham*

Belsay Castle, *Northumberland*

Berkhamsted Castle, *Hertfordshire*

Berwick-upon-Tweed Castle and Ramparts, *Northumberland*

Brougham Castle, *Cumbria*

Brough Castle, *Cumbria*

Castle Rising Castle, *Norfolk*

Farleigh Hungerford Castle, *Somerset*

Farnham Castle Keep, *Surrey*

Goodrich Castle, *Hereford & Worcester*

Helmsley Castle, *North Yorkshire*

Hurst Castle, *Hampshire*

Launceston Castle, *Cornwall*

Middleham Castle, *North Yorkshire*

Norham Castle, *Northumberland*

Nunney Castle, *Somerset*

Okehampton Castle, *Devon*

Orford Castle, *Suffolk*

Pickering Castle, *North Yorkshire*

Piel Castle, *Cumbria*

Portchester Castle, *Hampshire*

Portland Castle, *Dorset*

Prudhoe Castle, *Northumberland*

Restormel Castle, *Cornwall*

Rochester Castle, *Kent*

St Mawes Castle, *Cornwall*

Sherborne Old Castle, *Dorset*

Stokesay Castle, *Shropshire*

Tynemouth Castle, *Tyne & Wear*

Upnor Castle, *Kent*

Walmer Castle, *Kent*

Yarmouth Castle, *Isle of Wight*

ECCLESIASTICAL BUILDINGS

Binham Priory, *Norfolk*

Blackfriars, *Gloucestershire*

Brinkburn Priory, *Northumberland*

Buildwas Abbey, *Shropshire*

Bushmead Priory, *Bedfordshire*

Byland Abbey, *North Yorkshire*

Cleeve Abbey, *Somerset*

Easby Abbey, *North Yorkshire*

Egglestone Abbey, *Durham*

Furness Abbey, *Cumbria*

Goodshaw Chapel, *Lancashire*

Lanercost Priory, *Cumbria*

Lilleshall Abbey, *Shropshire*

Mount Grace Priory, *North Yorkshire*

Muchelney Abbey, *Somerset*

Netley Abbey, *Hampshire*

Odda's Chapel, Deerhurst, *Gloucestershire*

Roche Abbey, *South Yorkshire*

Rycote Chapel, *Oxfordshire*

St Augustine's Abbey, Canterbury, *Kent*

St Botolph's Priory, Colchester, *Essex*

St Mary's Church, Kempley, *Gloucestershire*

St Paul's Monastery, Jarrow, *Tyne & Wear*

St Mary's Church, Studley Royal, *North Yorkshire*

Thetford Priory, *Norfolk*

Titchfield Abbey, *Hampshire*

Tynemouth Priory, *Tyne & Wear*

Warkworth Hermitage, *Northumberland*

Wenlock Priory, *Shropshire*

SITES OPEN ALL THE YEAR ROUND

Acton Burnell Castle, *Shropshire*

Aldborough Roman Town, *North Yorkshire*

Appuldurcombe House, *Isle of Wight*

Ashby de la Zouch Castle, *Leicestershire*

Baconsthorpe Castle, *Norfolk*

Berkhamsted Castle, *Hertfordshire*

Berwick-upon-Tweed Fortifications, *Northumberland*

Binham Priory and Wayside Cross, *Norfolk*

Bishop's Waltham Palace, *Hampshire*

Bolsover Castle, *Derbyshire*

Boscobel House, *Shropshire*

Brough Castle, *Cumbria*

Brougham Castle, *Cumbria*

Buildwas Abbey, *Shropshire*

Burton Agnes Old Manor House, *Humberside*

Byland Abbey, *North Yorkshire*

Castlerigg Stone Circles, *Cumbria*

Castle Rising Castle, *Norfolk*

Cleeve Abbey, *Somerset*

Dover Castle, *Kent*

Easby Abbey, *North Yorkshire*

Egglestone Abbey, *Durham*

Eltham Palace, *Greater London*

Farleigh Hungerford Castle, *Somerset*

Furness Abbey, *Cumbria*

Goodrich Castle, *Hereford & Worcester*

Goodshaw Chapel, *Lancashire*

The Grange, Northington, *Hampshire*

Grimes Graves, *Norfolk*

Helmsley Castle, *North Yorkshire*

Jewel Tower, *London*

Jewry Wall, *Leicestershire*

Kirkham Priory, *North Yorkshire*

Launceston Castle, *Cornwall*

Longthorpe Tower, *Cambridgeshire*

Lullingstone Roman Villa, *Kent*

Marble Hill House, *Greater London*

Middleham Castle, *North Yorkshire*

Minster Lovell Hall, *Oxfordshire*

Mount Grace Priory, *North Yorkshire*

Muchelney Abbey, *Somerset*

Norham Castle, *Northumberland*

Nunney Castle, *Somerset*

Okehampton Castle, *Devon*

Old Merchant's House, *Norfolk*

Old Sarum, *Wiltshire*

Orford Castle, *Suffolk*

Pickering Castle, *North Yorkshire*

Piel Castle, *Cumbria*

Portchester Castle, *Hampshire*

Portland Castle, *Dorset*

Prudhoe Castle, *Northumberland*

Restormel Castle, *Cornwall*

Richborough Castle, *Kent*

Rochester Castle, *Kent*

Rushton Triangular Lodge, *Northamptonshire*

Rycote Chapel, *Oxfordshire*

Sherborne Old Castle, *Dorset*

St Augustine's Abbey, Canterbury, *Kent*

St Botolph's Priory, Colchester, *Essex*

St Mawes Castle, *Cornwall*

St Paul's Monastery, Jarrow, *Tyne & Wear*

Stanton Drew Stone Circles, *Avon*

Thetford Priory, *Norfolk*

Tynemouth Castle and Priory, *Tyne & Wear*

Walmer Castle, *Kent*

Wenlock Priory, *Shropshire*

Witley Court, *Hereford & Worcester*

Wroxeter Roman City, *Shropshire*

SITES WITH FREE ENTRY

Acton Burnell Castle, *Shropshire*

Baconsthorpe Castle, *Norfolk*

Berkhamsted Castle, *Hertfordshire*

Berwick-upon-Tweed Castle and Ramparts, *Northumberland*

Binham Priory and Wayside Cross, *Norfolk*

Burton Agnes Old Manor House, *Humberside*

Castlerigg Stone Circle, *Cumbria*

Castle Rising Castle, *Norfolk*

Egglestone Abbey, *Durham*

Eltham Palace, *Greater London*

Goodshaw Chapel, *Lancashire*

The Grange, Northington, *Hampshire*

Jewel Tower, *London*

Jewry Wall, *Leicestershire*

Marble Hill House, *Greater London*

Minster Lovell Hall, *Oxfordshire*

Mistley Towers, *Essex*

Netley Abbey, *Hampshire*

Nunney Castle, *Somerset*

Odda's Chapel, Deerhurst, *Gloucestershire*

Piel Castle, *Cumbria*

St Botolph's Priory, Colchester, *Essex*

St Paul's Monastery, Jarrow, *Tyne & Wear*

St Mary's Church, Kempley, *Gloucestershire*

St Mary's Church, Studley Royal, *North Yorkshire*

Thetford Priory, *Norfolk*

Witley Court, *Hereford & Worcester*

SPECIAL EVENTS AND ENTERTAINMENT

These sites all hold special events on certain dates throughout the year, ranging from medieval combat to traditional craft fairs, musical evenings to flower shows:

Ashby de la Zouch Castle, *Leicestershire*

Belsay Hall, *Northumberland*

Barnard Castle, *Durham*

Berwick-upon-Tweed Barracks, *Northumberland*

Blackfriars, *Gloucestershire*

Boscobel House, *Shropshire*

Castle Rising Castle, *Norfolk*

Farleigh Hungerford Castle, *Somerset*

Goodrich Castle, *Hereford & Worcester*

Launceston Castle, *Cornwall*

Marble Hill House, *Greater London*

Middleham Castle, *North Yorkshire*

Pickering Castle, *North Yorkshire*

Portchester Castle, *Hampshire*

Prudhoe Castle, *Northumberland*

Restormel Castle, *Cornwall*

Richborough Castle, *Kent*

Rycote Chapel, *Oxfordshire*

Tynemouth Castle and Priory, *Tyne & Wear*

Walmer Castle, *Kent*

Wenlock Priory, *Shropshire*

Wroxeter Roman City, *Shropshire*

GARDENS OF PARTICULAR INTEREST

Appuldurcombe House, *Isle of Wight*

Belsay Hall, Castle and Gardens, *Northumberland*

Boscobel House, *Shropshire*

St Mawes Castle, *Cornwall*

Stokesay Castle, *Shropshire*

Walmer Castle, *Kent*

Witley Court, *Hereford & Worcester*

Wrest Park House and Gardens, *Bedfordshire*

TOUR PLANNER
COUNTY MAPS

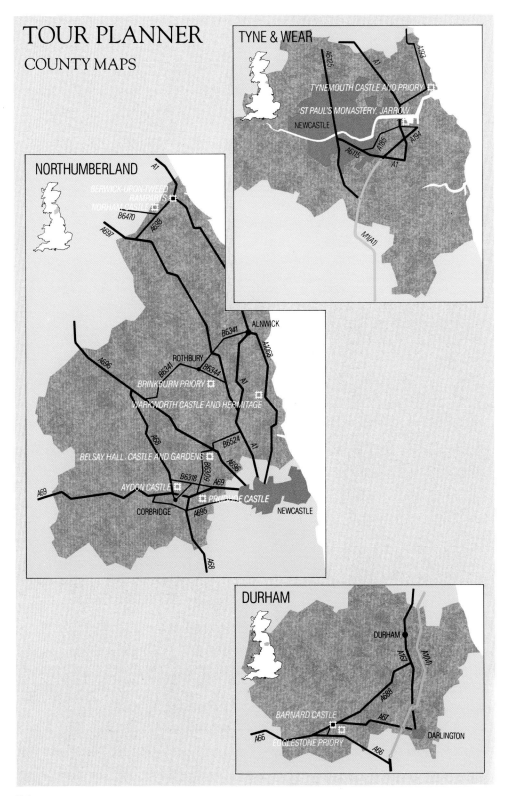

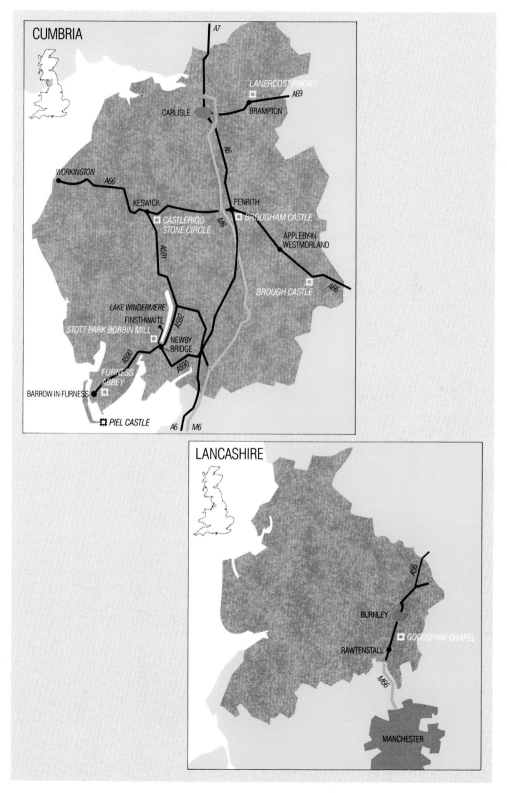

NORTH YORKSHIRE · HUMBERSIDE

RICHMOND
EASBY ABBEY
LEYBURN
MIDDLEHAM CASTLE
A1(M)
B6271
A19
A172
INGLEBY ARNCLIFFE
MOUNT GRACE PRIORY
A684
NORTHALLERTON
SCARBOROUGH
A61
A170
HELMSLEY CASTLE
PICKERING CASTLE
THIRSK
BYLAND ABBEY
COXWOLD
A6108
A169
A64
RIPON
ST MARY'S STUDLEY ROYAL
BOROUGHBRIDGE
KIRKHAM PRIORY
MALTON
BRIDLINGTON
A166
ALDBOROUGH ROMAN TOWN
B6265
GT. DRIFFIELD
BURTON AGNES MANOR
HARROGATE
A59
SKIPTON
YORK
A166
A1
A64
A19

SOUTH YORKSHIRE · DERBYSHIRE

M18
M1
A1(M)
DONCASTER
ROTHERHAM
MALTBY
A631
SHEFFIELD
ROCHE ABBEY
A632
CHESTERFIELD
BOLSOVER CASTLE
A1
A61
M1
DERBY

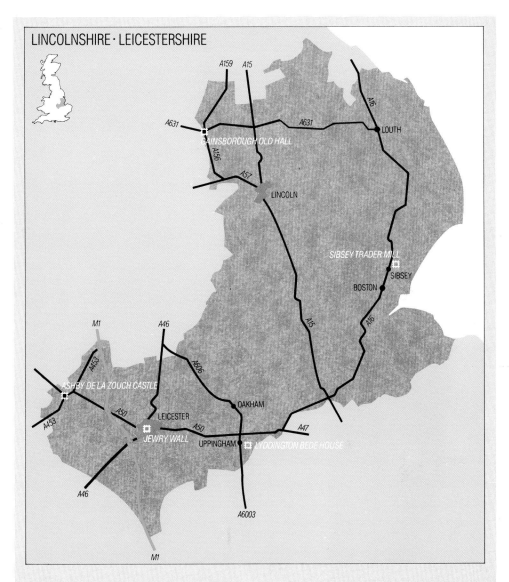

LINCOLNSHIRE · LEICESTERSHIRE

A159
A15
A16
A631
A631
LOUTH
GAINSBOROUGH OLD HALL
A156
A57
LINCOLN
SIBSEY TRADER MILL
SIBSEY
BOSTON
A15
A16
M1
A46
A453
A606
ASHBY DE LA ZOUCH CASTLE
A50
OAKHAM
LEICESTER
A453
A50
A47
JEWRY WALL
UPPINGHAM
LYDDINGTON BEDE HOUSE
A46
A6003
M1

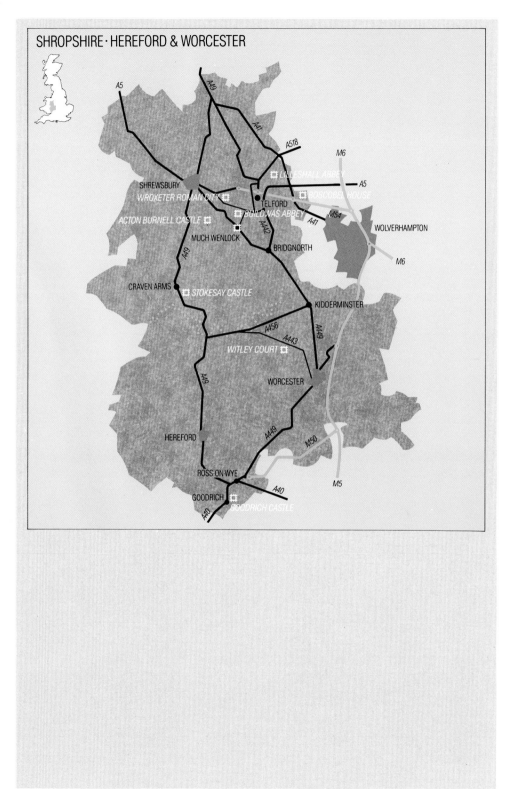

SHROPSHIRE · HEREFORD & WORCESTER

A5

A49

A41

A518

M6

LILLESHALL ABBEY

A5

SHREWSBURY

WROXETER ROMAN CITY

BOSCOBEL HOUSE

TELFORD

M54

ACTON BURNELL CASTLE

BUILDWAS ABBEY

A41

WOLVERHAMPTON

A442

MUCH WENLOCK

BRIDGNORTH

M6

A49

CRAVEN ARMS

STOKESAY CASTLE

KIDDERMINSTER

A449

A456

A443

WITLEY COURT

A49

WORCESTER

HEREFORD

A449

M50

ROSS-ON-WYE

M5

GOODRICH

A40

GOODRICH CASTLE

A40

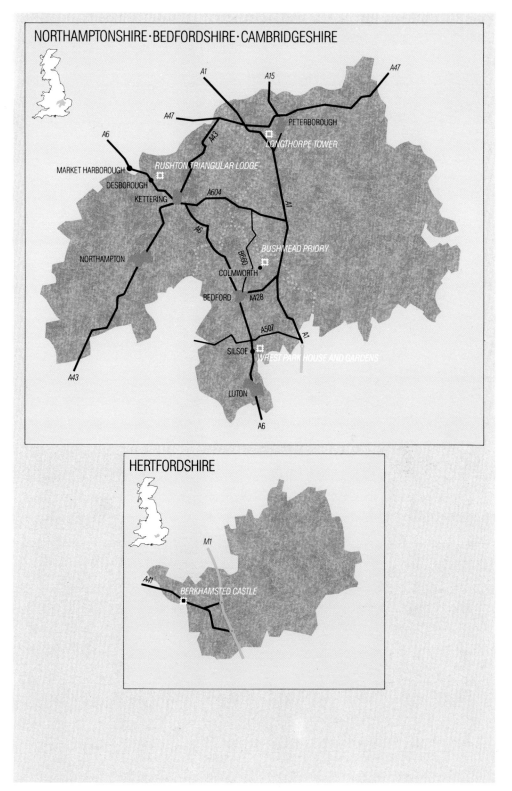

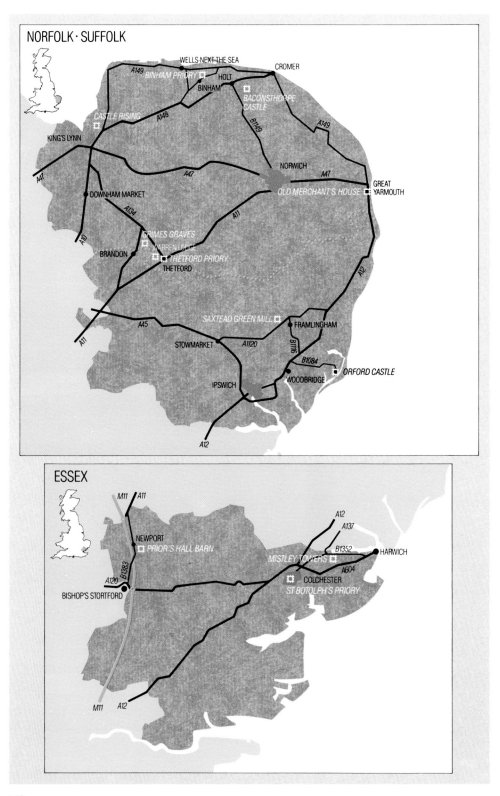

NORFOLK · SUFFOLK

WELLS-NEXT-THE-SEA
A149
BINHAM PRIORY
HOLT
BINHAM
CROMER
BACONSTHORPE CASTLE
CASTLE RISING
A148
B1149
A149
KING'S LYNN
A47
NORWICH
A47
DOWNHAM MARKET
OLD MERCHANT'S HOUSE
GREAT YARMOUTH
A134
A47
A11
A10
GRIMES GRAVES
WARREN LODGE
BRANDON
THETFORD PRIORY
THETFORD
A12
A45
SAXTEAD GREEN MILL
FRAMLINGHAM
A11
STOWMARKET
A1120
B1116
B1084
ORFORD CASTLE
IPSWICH
WOODBRIDGE
A12

ESSEX

M11
A11
NEWPORT
PRIOR'S HALL BARN
A12
A137
B1352
HARWICH
MISTLEY TOWERS
B1383
A120
A604
ST BOTOLPH'S PRIORY
COLCHESTER
BISHOP'S STORTFORD
M11
A12

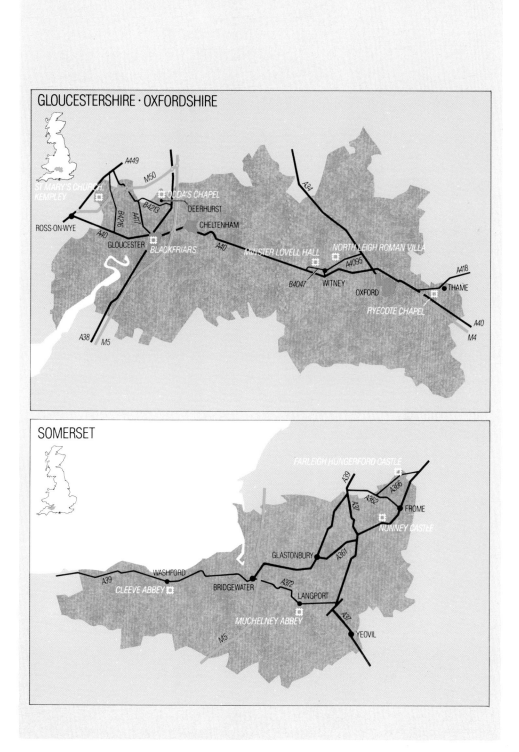

GLOUCESTERSHIRE · OXFORDSHIRE

A449
M50
A34
ST MARY'S CHURCH KEMPLEY
ODDA'S CHAPEL
DEERHURST
B4213
A417
B4216
ROSS-ON-WYE
A40
CHELTENHAM
GLOUCESTER
BLACKFRIARS
A40
MINSTER LOVELL HALL
NORTH LEIGH ROMAN VILLA
A4095
A418
WITNEY
B4047
THAME
OXFORD
RYECOTE CHAPEL
A38
M5
A40
M4

SOMERSET

FARLEIGH HUNGERFORD CASTLE
A39
A366
A362
A37
FROME
NUNNEY CASTLE
GLASTONBURY
A361
WASHFORD
CLEEVE ABBEY
BRIDGEWATER
A372
LANGPORT
A39
MUCHELNEY ABBEY
A37
YEOVIL
M5

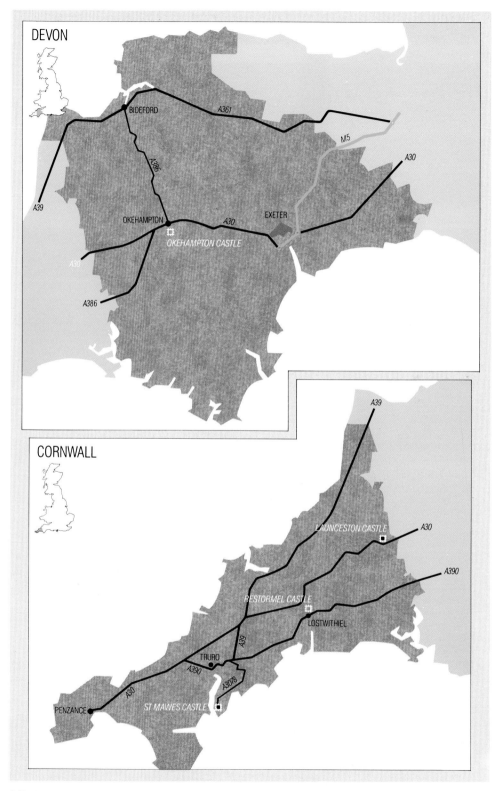

DEVON

BIDEFORD

A361

M5

A30

A39

A386

OKEHAMPTON

A30

EXETER

OKEHAMPTON CASTLE

A30

A386

CORNWALL

A39

LAUNCESTON CASTLE

A30

A390

RESTORMEL CASTLE

LOSTWITHIEL

A39

TRURO

A390

A39

A30

A3078

PENZANCE

ST MAWES CASTLE

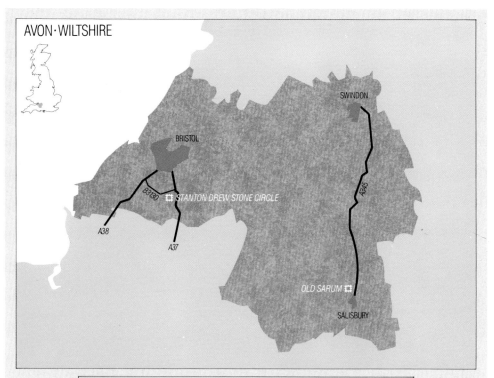

AVON·WILTSHIRE

SWINDON

BRISTOL

B3130

□ STANTON DREW STONE CIRCLE

A38

A37

A346

OLD SARUM □

SALISBURY

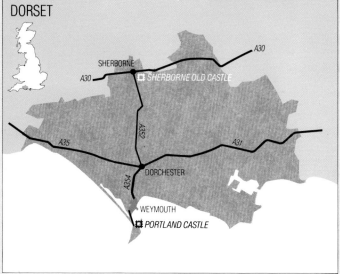

DORSET

A30

SHERBORNE

A30

□ SHERBORNE OLD CASTLE

A35

A352

A31

DORCHESTER

A354

WEYMOUTH

□ PORTLAND CASTLE

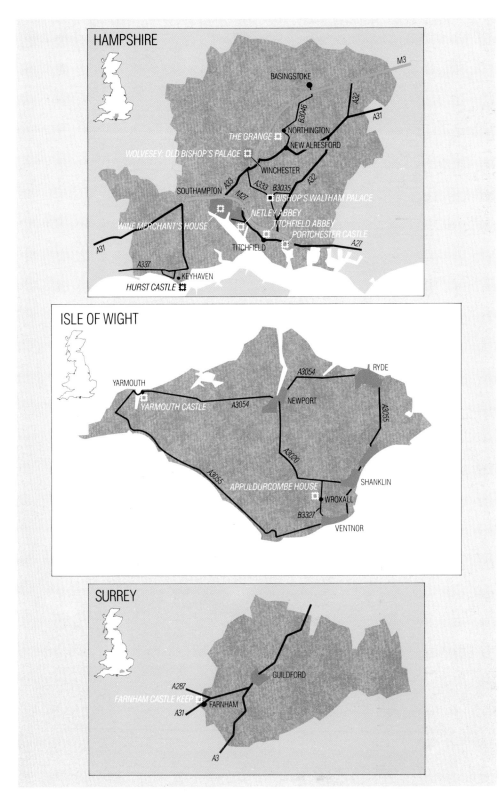

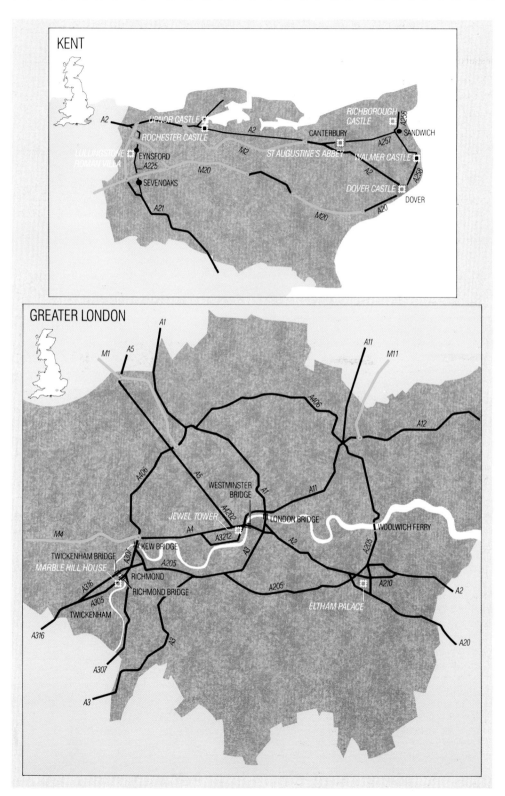

KENT

UPNOR CASTLE
A2
ROCHESTER CASTLE
A2
CANTERBURY
A257
SANDWICH
LULLINGSTONE
ROMAN VILLA
EYNSFORD
A225
M2
ST AUGUSTINE'S ABBEY
WALMER CASTLE
M20
A2
A258
SEVENOAKS
DOVER CASTLE
A21
M20
A20
DOVER

RICHBOROUGH
CASTLE
A256

GREATER LONDON

A1
M1
A5
A11
M11
A406
A12
A406
A5
WESTMINSTER
BRIDGE
A1
A11
JEWEL TOWER
A4202
A4
A3212
LONDON BRIDGE
WOOLWICH FERRY
M4
KEW BRIDGE
A3
A2
A205
TWICKENHAM BRIDGE
A307
MARBLE HILL HOUSE
A205
A210
A2
RICHMOND
A316
A205
RICHMOND BRIDGE
A305
ELTHAM PALACE
TWICKENHAM
A3
A316
A307
A20
A3

THE ROYAL HOUSES OF ENGLAND

1066 TO THE PRESENT DAY

The Norman Conquest

Edward the Confessor, King of Anglo-Saxon England, died without heirs in 1066, leaving two rival claimants to the throne: his brother-in-law Harold, Earl of Wessex, and his cousin William, Duke of Normandy. Harold was elected king, but in a shipwreck off the coast of Normandy two years earlier had been forced to swear to support William's claim. Harold's exiled brother Tostig, Earl of Northumberland, and Harald Hardrade, King of Norway, seized the opportunity to invade the north, but were killed by Harold at the battle of Stamford Bridge, at the very moment that the Normans landed on the Channel coast. Harold turned south to face William, but his depleted force was defeated at the battle of Hastings.

Domesday

Following the Norman Conquest, William acted quickly to ensure control over his new kingdom: in 1069 a serious rebellion in the north was put down by the 'harrying of the north' – devastation and depopulation across a swathe of country between Durham and York. William asserted his power by introducing the feudal system and in 1086 everyone who held lands directly from the king swore an oath of loyalty to him. In the same year royal commissioners completed a survey of the kingdom: citizens of every village and county were asked on oath to give information on the size, resources and ownership of every strip of land. This information was invaluable to the king for administrative purposes and to assess the wealth of his new kingdom for taxation. It has proved an equally valuable historical record.

Civil Wars in King Stephen's Reign

Henry I was the third son of William the Conqueror and succeeded his brother William Rufus to the throne. When Henry's son died in 1120, his daughter Matilda was accepted as his heir. Matilda was married to Geoffrey of Anjou for protection from the claims of Stephen of Boulogne, the son of Henry I's sister Adela. When Henry I died in 1135, Stephen seized his chance to take the crown. This led to a dynastic quarrel with Matilda, which lasted until 1135. Matilda invaded in 1139 and two years later captured Stephen at the battle of Lincoln: she reigned for a short time, but was driven out by a popular uprising, when Stephen regained the throne. Matilda's son Henry of Anjou landed in 1135 to pursue his claim and a compromise was negotiated, whereby Stephen should acknowledge Henry of Anjou as his heir.

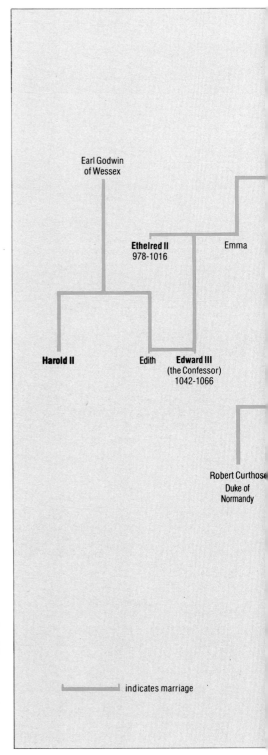

Earl Godwin of Wessex

Ethelred II 978-1016

Emma

Harold II

Edith

Edward III (the Confessor) 1042-1066

Robert Curthose Duke of Normandy

⎿▬▬▬▬⏌ indicates marriage

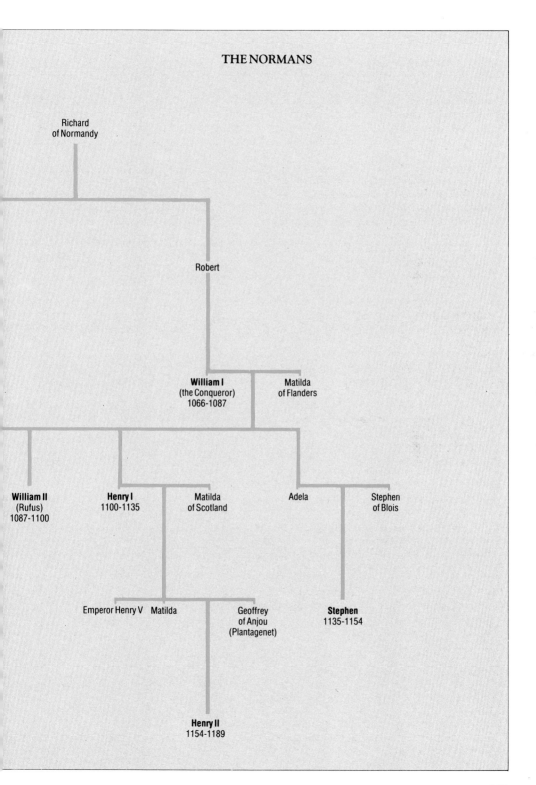

THE NORMANS

Richard
of Normandy

Robert

William I
(the Conqueror)
1066-1087

Matilda
of Flanders

William II
(Rufus)
1087-1100

Henry I
1100-1135

Matilda
of Scotland

Adela

Stephen
of Blois

Emperor Henry V   Matilda

Geoffrey
of Anjou
(Plantagenet)

Stephen
1135-1154

Henry II
1154-1189

The Hundred Years' War

At the accession of Henry II, the crown of England claimed lands in all of western France, either by inheritance or through Henry's marriage to Eleanor of Aquitaine. In addition, the Plantagenets had their own claims to the throne of France and were in conflict with the French over their support of Scotland. In 1337 Edward III was provoked by attacks on his French lands into declaring himself to be King of France; this sparked off a sporadic series of battles and campaigns lasting over a hundred years. In 1346 the English won the battle of Crécy, but the first phase of the war ended in 1360, when Edward gave up his claim to the French throne. That claim was renewed in 1415 by Henry V, who won the famous victory at Agincourt. Under his son Henry VI, however, the English fared badly and the French gained inspiration from Joan of Arc, who led the French forces in 1429. She was burnt as a witch by the English two years later, but by 1451 all of France, except Calais, had been recaptured by the French.

William   Henry

Eleanor
of Castile

Joan

—————— indicates marriage

THE PLANTAGENETS

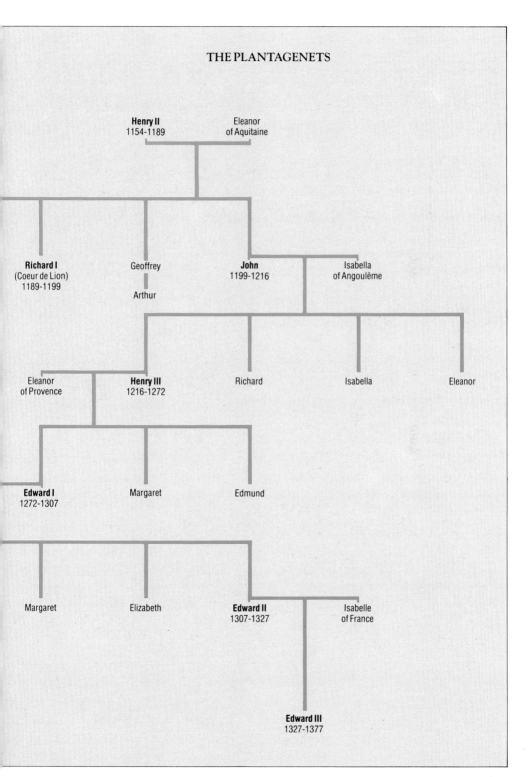

Henry II
1154-1189

Eleanor
of Aquitaine

Richard I
(Coeur de Lion)
1189-1199

Geoffrey

Arthur

John
1199-1216

Isabella
of Angoulême

Eleanor
of Provence

Henry III
1216-1272

Richard

Isabella

Eleanor

Edward I
1272-1307

Margaret

Edmund

Margaret

Elizabeth

Edward II
1307-1327

Isabelle
of France

Edward III
1327-1377

The Rise of the House of Lancaster

Richard II succeeded his grandfather, Edward II, in 1377 as his father Edward, the Black Prince, was already dead. He was only ten years old at the time of his accession and during his minority his uncle John of Gaunt, Duke of Lancaster, was effective ruler of the country. In 1389 Richard II assumed control of the government, and from 1397 increasingly tried to rule autocratically. He was incensed by a demand from Parliament for financial accountability and forced Parliament to vote him an income for life, imposing heavy taxation. After the death of John of Gaunt in 1399, his exiled son, Henry Bolingbroke, conspired for the throne. Bolingbroke landed while Richard was in Ireland and forced him to abdicate. Richard was sent to the Tower of London, where he died mysteriously in 1400, the year after Bolingbroke was crowned Henry IV, the first of the Lancastrians.

The Wars of the Roses

Henry VI, the grandson of Henry IV, was fitfully insane and during the periods of his insanity the country was governed by a council headed by Richard, Duke of York. In 1455 Henry recovered and the Duke of York was removed from the council; for the next thirty years the Houses of Lancaster and York, both descended from Edward III, were to be in conflict over the throne. Richard of York was killed at the battle of Westfield in 1460, but the following year his 19-year-old son defeated the Lancastrians and was crowned king, as Edward IV. Henry VI died ten years later in the Tower of London, probably murdered. Edward himself died prematurely in 1483 and was succeeded by his young son Edward V. He in turn was deposed by his uncle Richard, Duke of Gloucester – the hunchbacked Richard III. The continuous wars culminated in the decisive battle of Bosworth, at which Richard was defeated and killed by Henry Tudor, Duke of Richmond and a descendant of John of Gaunt by his second marriage. Henry Tudor succeeded in uniting the two warring Houses by marrying Elizabeth of York, the daughter of Edward IV, and ruled as Henry VIII, first of the Tudor monarchs.

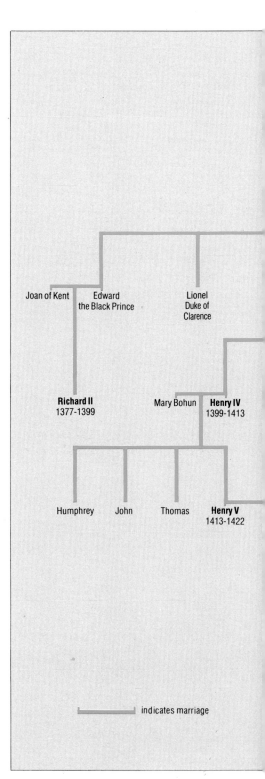

THE HOUSES OF LANCASTER AND YORK

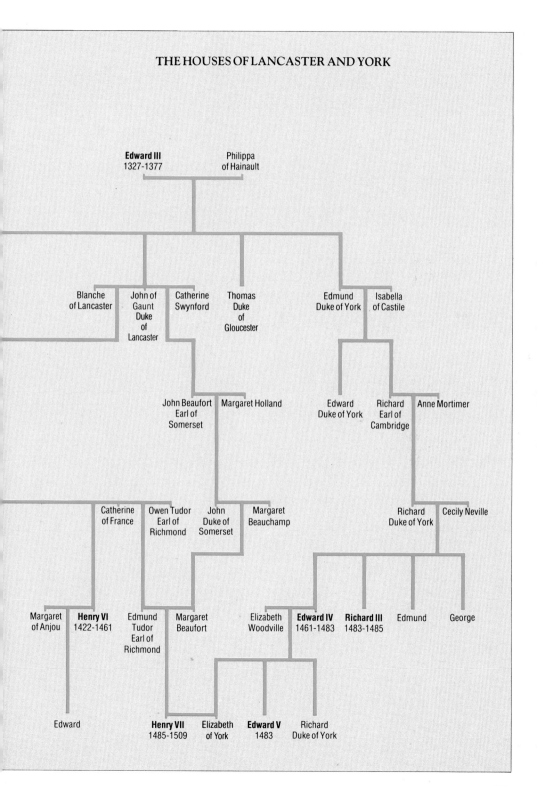

The Reformation and the Dissolution of the Monasteries

In Germany the Reformation was a popular movement intent on reforming the corrupt Catholic Church, but in England it began with Henry VIII's desire to divorce his first wife Catherine of Aragon, marry Anne Boleyn and produce a son and heir. Although the Pope refused to annul the marriage to Catherine, Henry married Anne Boleyn in 1533. He was excommunicated from the Church, but the following year the Act of Supremacy was passed in England to make him Supreme Head of the Church of England. Under the pretext of Reformation, Henry VIII was able to disband many monastic houses who controlled extensive lands, which then fell to the king. This process, known as the dissolution of the monasteries, began in 1536 and continued over several years.

The Union of England and Scotland

In 1502 Henry VII married his eldest daughter to James IV, King of Scotland. Henry's son, Henry VIII, had three children (Edward VI, Mary and Elizabeth I), all of whom died without producing any heirs, male or female, and after the death of Elizabeth the succession passed to James VI of Scotland, who thus also became James I of England. James VI and I was a great-great-grandson to Henry VII and both of his parents were grandchildren of Henry VIII's sister, Margaret: his mother from Margaret's first marriage to James IV of Scotland; his father from Margaret's second marriage to Archibald Douglas. The Union of the two kingdoms in 1603 occured solely through the person of James VI and I: it was not until the Act of Union of May 1707 that Great Britain was formally created, with a single monarch and a single Parliament.

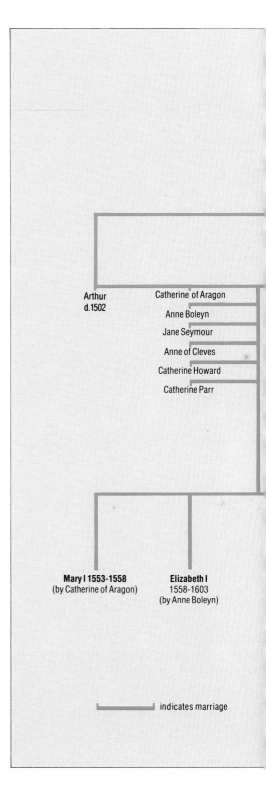

Arthur
d.1502

Catherine of Aragon

Anne Boleyn

Jane Seymour

Anne of Cleves

Catherine Howard

Catherine Parr

Mary I 1553-1558
(by Catherine of Aragon)

Elizabeth I
1558-1603
(by Anne Boleyn)

━━━━━━┛ indicates marriage

THE TUDORS

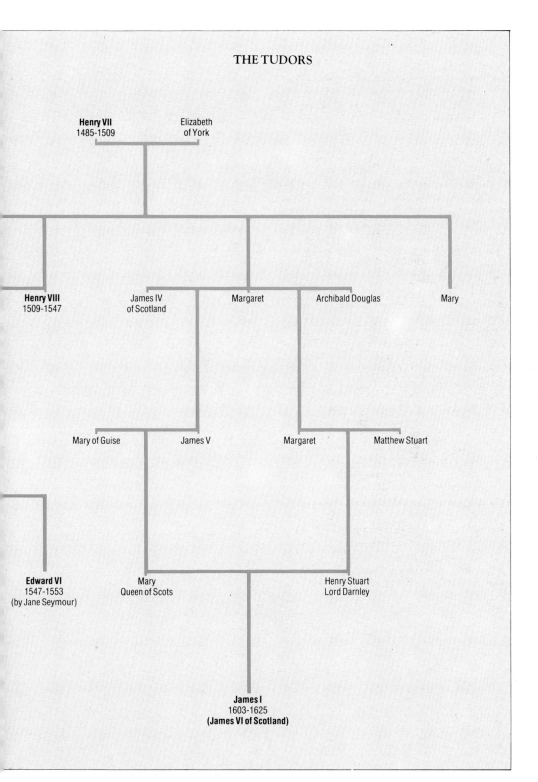

Henry VII
1485-1509

Elizabeth
of York

Henry VIII
1509-1547

James IV
of Scotland

Margaret

Archibald Douglas

Mary

Mary of Guise

James V

Margaret

Matthew Stuart

Edward VI
1547-1553
(by Jane Seymour)

Mary
Queen of Scots

Henry Stuart
Lord Darnley

James I
1603-1625
(James VI of Scotland)

The Civil War

The Stuart kings believed in the Divine Right of Kings, which caused sharp conflict with the requirements of Parliament on the subjects of taxation, religion and the control of the army. Charles I managed to rule for 11 years (1629-40) without calling Parliament, but in time was forced to do so as he desperately needed money to fight the Scots. Over the next two years he made various concessions to Parliament until the only disagreement was over who should control the army: the members of Parliament could not trust Charles not to use the army against them, and in 1642 they raised their own army against the king. The Royalist side won early victories, but the Parliamentarians (Roundheads), under Oliver Cromwell, eventually defeated the king with the help of the Scots. Charles I was tried and executed by Parliament in 1649 and the Commonwealth formed. The following year his son and heir landed in Scotland and was crowned Charles II. He advanced southwards but was defeated at the battle of Worcester by Cromwell. Cromwell became Lord Protector of the Commonwealth in 1653, which he remained until his death in 1658.

The Restoration

Following the execution of Charles I, there remained the problem of what form the constitution of England should take. Cromwell was made Lord Protector of the Commonwealth in 1653, but three years later he refused the title of king. After his death in 1658, Cromwell's son took over the title of Lord Protector, but there followed a series of disputes between the army and Parliament and Richard was forced to resign. In April 1660, Charles II issued from exile the Declaration of Breda, proclaiming an amnesty, freedom of conscience and confirmation of estates confiscated during the Civil War. This was accepted by Parliament and Charles entered London as king on 29 May 1660.

Henry d. 1612

Charles II
1660-1685

Henrietta

indicates marriage

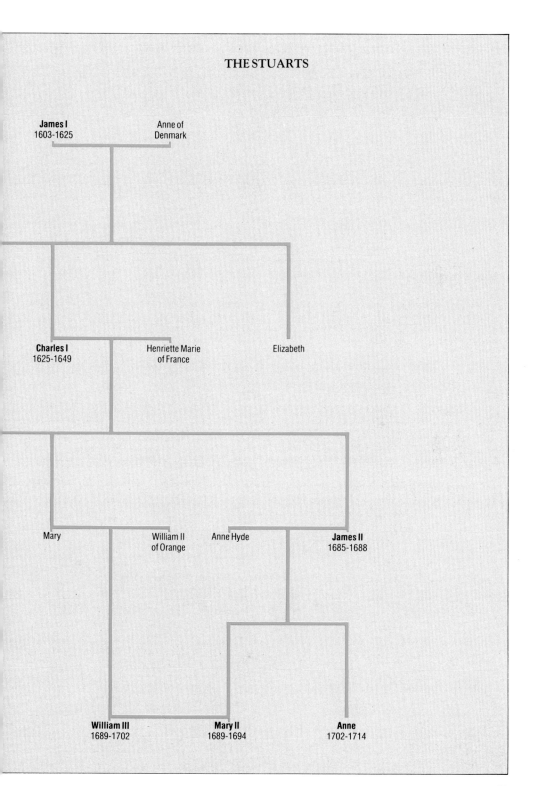

THE STUARTS

James I
1603-1625

Anne of
Denmark

Charles I
1625-1649

Henriette Marie
of France

Elizabeth

Mary

William II
of Orange

Anne Hyde

James II
1685-1688

William III
1689-1702

Mary II
1689-1694

Anne
1702-1714

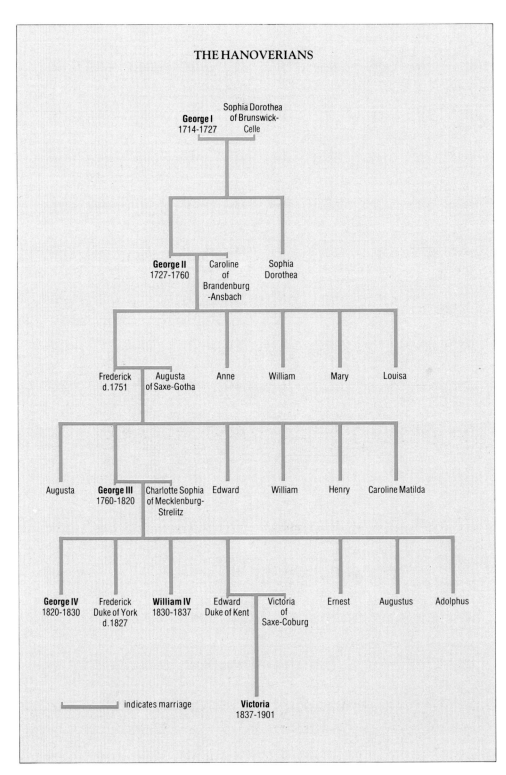

THE HANOVERIANS

George I 1714-1727 — Sophia Dorothea of Brunswick-Celle

George II 1727-1760 — Caroline of Brandenburg-Ansbach

Sophia Dorothea

Frederick d.1751 — Augusta of Saxe-Gotha

Anne

William

Mary

Louisa

Augusta

George III 1760-1820 — Charlotte Sophia of Mecklenburg-Strelitz

Edward

William

Henry

Caroline Matilda

George IV 1820-1830

Frederick Duke of York d.1827

William IV 1830-1837

Edward Duke of Kent — Victoria of Saxe-Coburg

Ernest

Augustus

Adolphus

▬▬▬▬ indicates marriage

Victoria 1837-1901

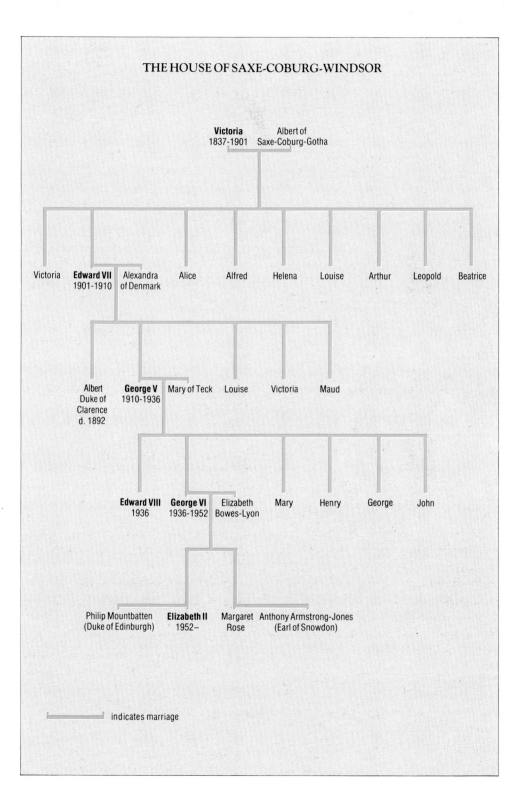

THE HOUSE OF SAXE-COBURG-WINDSOR

Victoria · Albert of
1837-1901 · Saxe-Coburg-Gotha

Victoria · **Edward VII** · Alexandra · Alice · Alfred · Helena · Louise · Arthur · Leopold · Beatrice
1901-1910 · of Denmark

Albert · **George V** · Mary of Teck · Louise · Victoria · Maud
Duke of · 1910-1936
Clarence
d. 1892

Edward VIII · **George VI** · Elizabeth · Mary · Henry · George · John
1936 · 1936-1952 · Bowes-Lyon

Philip Mountbatten · **Elizabeth II** · Margaret · Anthony Armstrong-Jones
(Duke of Edinburgh) · 1952– · Rose · (Earl of Snowdon)

▬▬▬▬ indicates marriage

GLOSSARY

abbey Monastery or convent ruled by an abbott or abbess; the buildings, especially the church, of a former abbey.

ambulatory Semicircular aisle inside the east end (apse) of a church behind the altar.

angle turret Small tower at the angle of a castle wall.

apse Semicircular or polygonal end to the chancel or chapel of a church; a similar feature in a secular building.

arcading Series of arches.

arched brace Curved subsidiary timber in roof, strengthening the frame.

ashlar Squared, hewn stone or masonry in regular courses.

Augustinian Pertaining to or belonging to the order of monks founded by St Augustine (AD354-430).

bailey (see motte and bailey).

barbican Outwork to a gateway.

bargeboard Projecting wooden attachments to the verges of a roof, used to hide the ends of horizontal roof timbers.

baroque Florid style of late Renaissance architecture prevalent in England in the late-seventeenth and early-eighteenth centuries.

bar tracery Decorative work in the upper part of a window, formed by the branching of the verticals (mullions).

bastion Projection at the angle of a fortification, enabling defending soldiers to use flanking fire.

battlements Indented parapet for defence.

Benedictine Pertaining to or belonging to the order founded by St Benedict in AD529.

boss Projecting ornament, concealing intersection of ribs in a vault or roof.

Bronze Age Prehistoric period when metals such as copper and bronze came into use (in Europe c.2000-1000BC).

bull's eye window Small oval window, the long axis being horizontal.

buttery Store-room in a medieval house for ales, liquors and provisions.

buttress Stone or brick projection designed to support a wall.

canon Rule or decree of the Church; clergyman who is a member of the chapter or staff of a Cathedral.

canonical hour Time of day appointed by canon law for a religious service.

casement Window hinged on one of its edges, so as to open inwards or outwards.

cell One of a number of small chambers inhabited by monks in a monastery.

chancel Eastern continuation of the nave of a church, usually containing the altar and reserved for the clergy and choir.

chapterhouse Room in which monks met daily, to discuss business and hear a chapter of the monastic rule.

chevron A three-dimensional V-shaped motif. The zigzag pattern is characteristic of Norman decorative moulding.

Cistercian Pertaining to or belonging to the monastic order founded at Citeaux in 1098 by Robert, abbot of Molesme.

Cluniac Pertaining to or belonging to the monastic order of Cluny founded in AD910 in Burgundy, France.

coffering Decoration of ceiling, vault or arch with sunken panels.

Compline The last service of the day, completing the services of the canonical hours; the hour of that service.

confessional A stall or box in which a priest hears confessions.

corbel A stone or timber projection from the face of a wall intended to support a shaft, chimney or beam.

cruciform In the form of a cross, cross-shaped.

crypt A vault beneath the main floor of a church.

curtain wall The enclosing wall of a castle, usually punctuated by towers or bastions.

cusp Small projecting point at the intersection of arcs in the tracery of Gothic windows and arches.

Distemper Paint in which the colouring is mixed with white or yolk of egg and size, often used in the decoration of walls; to paint with distemper.

dorter Monastic dormitory.

drawbridge A hinged or pivoted bridge which can be raised on the approach of an enemy.

dungeon A dark deep vault, often used as a prison, in a castle.

Early English A stylistic phase of English Gothic architecture covering the thirteenth century. It follows the Norman and precedes the Decorated. A characteristic feature is the lancet window without tracery.

Elizabethan Belonging to, or in the style of the period of Queen Elizabeth I (1558-1603).

ermine Heraldic motif on a shield, consisting of a white background with conventional black spots, representing the fur of an ermine.

facade The face or front of a building.

font Receptacle, usually of stone, designed to hold the holy water which is used at the sacrament of baptism.

forum Public square or meeting place in Roman city used for court or tribunal.

frater Monastery refectory or dining room.

fresco Technique of wall decoration using one of two methods: in true fresco colours are applied to wet plaster and fuse with it as it dries; in dry fresco colour is applied to plaster that has already dried.

Georgian Generally, the period of the reign of the four Georges (1714-1830). In architecture, the style of the Neo-Palladians, inspired by sixteenth century Venetian, Andrea Palladio, and introduced to England by Inigo Jones in 1615.

Gothic Style of architecture prevalent in Western Europe from the twelfth to the fifteenth century, of which the chief characteristic was the pointed arch.

groin vault A type of arched roof or ceiling which takes its name from the arched diagonals, or groins, formed by the intersection of two barrel (semi-circular) vaults at right angles.

grotesque A form of decoration composed of fanciful animal and human forms, fruit and flowers.

hammerbeam roof One in which the tie beam is cut short to form hammerbeams which, standing on wall posts, themselves support hammer posts and arched braces to a collar.

henge Neolithic or Bronze Age ceremonial site, circular in plan, surrounded by bank and external ditch, with one or more entrances and such internal features as standing stones, timber buildings or burial cairns.

hypocaust A hollow space extending under the floor of Roman buildings in which the heat from a furnace was circulated.

impost Upper course of pilaster, pillar or pier from which an arch springs.

Indulgence Remission of punishment due according to Roman Catholicism, especially in Purgatory.

Ionic Type of column invented by the Greeks (c.650BC), consisting of a base, fluted pillar and volutes.

Jacobean A style of architecture predominant during the reign of James I (1603-25); evolving from the Elizabethan style, but characterized by purer classical forms, and the influence of Inigo Jones.

keep Fortified inner tower of a castle, which could serve as living quarters, either permanently or during a siege; also called a donjon.

lancet window Long narrow window with pointed head, characteristic of the thirteenth century.

leaded lights Panes of glass set in small grooved bars of lead to form a window.

limewash A mixture of lime and water used for coating walls.

linenfold panelling Tudor decoration, with appearance of folds of linen, laid vertically in a panel.

machicolations Openings in the floor of a projecting parapet or fighting gallery, through which missiles could be directed at an enemy.

manor Mansion of a lord or principal house of an estate.

Matins One of the canonical hours, properly a midnight service; morning service in the Church of England since the Reformation.

mauseoleum A building designed to contain one or more tombs.

medieval Pertaining to or characteristic of the Middle Ages (c.AD500-1500)

moat A deep, wide ditch surrounding a castle, house or town and usually filled with water.

monastery A secluded place of residence for a community of monks living under religious vows.

motte and bailey Artificial circular mound (motte) and courtyard (bailey) of a castle, characteristic of early Norman castles.

moulding Ornamental outline or shaping of a decorative feature.

nave The main body or central aisle of a church.

neo-classical A new classical style of architecture and decoration dominant in Europe c. 1760-90, which derived from ancient Greek and Roman monuments.

newel Central pillar round which the steps of a circular staircase wind.

Nonconformist A member of a religious body which refused to conform to the doctrine of the established church, the Church of England.

Norman The post-Conquest style of architecture current in England during the eleventh and twelfth centuries. Arches were semicircular, vaults were barrel-roofed but towers were mostly square.

oriel window Bay window projecting from an upper storey.

Palladian The architecture of Andrea Palladio (1508-80) and later sixteenth century Venice, introduced to England by Inigo Jones.

parapet A low protective wall on a bridge, gallery, balcony or above the cornice of a building.

pavilion An ornamental pleasure house in a park or garden, or, if part of a larger building, distinctively treated to set it apart, as the wings or central portion of a long facade.

Perpendicular The period of English architecture of the fourteenth and fifteenth centuries, characterized by the strong vertical lines of its tracery.

pinnacle A pyramidal or conical ornament used to terminate a gable, buttress or the angle of a parapet.

portcullis Iron-shod wooden grating, a movable gate for defence, rising or falling in vertical grooves in the jambs of a gateway.

postern A small secondary entrance, sometimes concealed, usually at the rear of the castle.

Premonstratensian Pertaining to or belonging to the order of monks founded by St Norbert at Prémontré near Laon in France in 1119; a member of a corresponding order of nuns.

Prime The second canonical hour of the Western Church, usually fixed at daybreak.

Puritan A member of the party of English protestants in the sixteenth and seventeenth centuries who did not approve of Roman Catholic practices within the Church of England.

quire Part of a church where services are sung; choir stalls.

ramparts A protective earth or stone wall, with or without a parapet, surrounding a castle or fortified place.

refectory The dining hall of a monastery, sometimes called the frater.

reredorter Communal privy situated at the back of a monastery dormitory.

rib vaulting Framework of arched ribs supporting a vault.

Romanesque Architectural style of the Norman period prior to the rise of Gothic architecture.

satyr mask Portrayal of a satyr, one of a class of woodland gods or demons, partly human and partly bestial, supposed to be the companions of Bacchus.

slighting Levelling with the ground.

solar Private upper room, leading off the great hall of a manor house.

Terce The third of the canonical hours, ending at 9am.

timber-framed crown post roof One in which the main support is provided by a crown post standing centrally on a tie beam, supporting a collar purlin and generally also braced to one of the collars.

trefoil Three small arc openings in Gothic tracery separated by cusps.

transept The transverse arm of a cruciform church.

vault An arched roof or ceiling.

Vespers The sixth of the canonical hours, sung towards evening.

ward Bailey or courtyard of a castle.

wooden trenching A wide groove in one timber to receive the whole width of another.

woolsack Large package or bale of wool.